The contributors to the book are:

Geoffrey Agnew: Art dealer and critic.

Michael Ayrton: Painter, sculptor, author, theatre designer, and illustrator.

L. D. Ettlinger: Durning Lawrence Professor of the History of Art, London.

Andrew Forge: Painter and critic.

Sir Philip Hendy: Director of the National Gallery, London.

David Piper: Director of the National Portrait Gallery, London.

David Talbot Rice: Watson-Gordon Professor of the History of Fine Art, Edinburgh.

Bryan Robertson: Art critic and Director of the Whitechapel Art Gallery, London.

Sir John Summerson: Historian of architecture and Curator of Sir John Soane's Museum, London.

Ellis Waterhouse: Barber Professor of Fine Arts, and Director of the Barber Institute, Birmingham.

Carel Weight: Painter, Professor of Painting, Royal College of Art, London.

Enjoying Paintings

Pelican Book A624

Enjoying

Paintings

Edited with
an introduction by
David Piper
with twelve colour
plates and
seventy-four
black-and-white
illustrations
Published by
Penguin Books

Penguin Books Ltd, Harmondsworth, Middlesex, England
Penguin Books Inc., 3300 Clipper Mill Road, Baltimore 11, Md, U.S.A.
Penguin Books Pty Ltd, Ringwood, Victoria, Australia

Enjoying Paintings first published 1964

Copyright © Penguin Books, 1964

Made and printed in Great Britain by Balding + Mansell Ltd, Wisbech

Set in Monotype Times and Monotype Grotesque

Contents

Acknowledgement. The publishers gratefully acknowledge the help and collaboration of the B.B.C. in the preparation of this book, and especially for their help in providing the material for the illustrations and for the loan of the colour transparencies for ten of the main colour plates. Acknowledgements are also due to the contributors for allowing the use of the texts of their broadcasts and for amending them for this publication.

Foreword

In 1960 the B.B.C. started as an experiment a series of broadcasts called 'Painting of the Month'; in this, on the first Sunday of each month, a speaker discussed a painting that had some especial appeal to him. The choice was therefore entirely personal, and only limited by the proviso that any picture chosen should normally be available to his listeners in a public collection in Great Britain, or in a private house open to the public. This book is composed of a selection from the talks given in the first two years of this series, including one from each of the twelve contributors, whose professions include those of curator, art-historian, critic, professional painter, art-teacher, art-dealer, and novelist (some of them of course work in several of these capacities). No programme is offered; this is an anthology of essays on pictures which a dozen people like. In my choice however I have tried to cover as wide a range as the original material allowed, and I hope that together these essays may prove useful, especially to a non-specialist public, as pleasurable exercises in the art of seeing.

Any picture of importance is infinitely more than a passing easiness on the eye. Indeed, no great art is easy; the entry into it, and the exploration of it by the eye and the mind, by the imagination and the senses, can make heavy demands on the spectator's sympathy and knowledge, on his tenacity and energy even. I am sure none of the contributors to this book would claim that their own approach to these paintings is either exhaustive or the only one; but, while everyone develops his own technique of looking and of ordering the experience, examples of how other people do it may well stimulate and enrich this process – I, at least, have learnt a great deal from my fellow-contributors in the course of preparing this edition, even when on particular points I may not have been in sympathy with them.

In the B.B.C. series, each talk was preceded by the issue of a printed pamphlet to those who subscribed to the series; each pamphlet contained a number of reproductions (all repeated in this volume), together with some notes. The latter were intended, I believe, to provide a more purely factual background to the general survey given in the talk, but they were in fact handled in widely differing manner by the various contributors. They are reprinted here in considerably condensed form, after each essay; naturally there was usually some duplication of material in each essay and its notes. A great deal of this has been cut for the purposes of this edition, but readers will find that some repetition unavoidably remains.

Introduction

A passage from E. M. Forster may serve as text. Near the opening of
A Room with a View, we are with the heroine, Lucy, in the church of
Santa Croce in Florence –

*Of course, it must be a wonderful building. But how like a barn! And
how very cold! Of course, it contained frescoes by Giotto, in the presence of whose tactile values she was capable of feeling what was
proper. But who was to tell her which they were? She walked about
disdainfully, unwilling to be enthusiastic over monuments of uncertain
authorship or date. There was no one even to tell her which, of all the
sepulchral slabs that paved the naves and transepts, was the one that was
really beautiful, the one that had been most praised by Mr Ruskin. . . .*

That was written about 1908. Ruskin had been dead eight years,
but still was relevant to the desires of a young lady interested in art,
though she has clearly also been reading a more up-to-date author,
Bernard Berenson, from whom she has become aware that 'tactile
values' exist. But it is still 1908. Let a war pass and a civilization
almost founder – after the war, the eternal Lucy will be back in
Santa Croce. If diligent, she will still have read Berenson but perhaps not Ruskin, and in addition she may have read Roger Fry and
Clive Bell, and may urgently require, besides the comforts of
'tactile values', those of 'significant form'. Let another war pass,
and, though many things founder, Santa Croce does not. In the
nineteen-sixties (to the time of writing, at least) it is still there, and
there, in the season, you will find young Englishwomen who might
still be Lucies, though they appear in various guises. She may even
by now be a specialist in art, not only aware of which are the Giottos
but with a firm and reasoned opinion of whether they are really by
Giotto or not – she may even be such a specialist that she may be
almost unable to see them – 'not my period, dear'. At the other end
of the scale of informed opinion, there may be the suburban Lucy
who has come with her parents in a bus tour, has done Paris, Lyons,

Milan, Venice, and now two days for Florence, of which five minutes for the Giottos; she may often be recognized by a stunned daze of the face. In the last seven days or so, she has been directed firmly to what is what; in the Louvre perhaps, led by her guide from the Winged Victory almost clear through to the Mona Lisa in one ruthless swoop, past rows of pictures across whose fronts the guide draws relative unimportance like a blind. She is suffering – from wind, the result of a combination of an unaccustomed kind of food with jack-knifed hours in the motor-coach; from the discovery that the stones of Florence are harder on the feet than any in the world; perhaps even from travel-blindness, which occurs when the dizzy voyager, unable to bear any longer the unremitting volleys of strange sights, retracts his eyes like snails' and will only recognize objects of international common currency, like the pigeons in St Mark's Square which are clearly also visiting from Trafalgar Square, or a cat asleep in a shop-window, or a child's laugh, or a Coca-Cola bottle.

If especially doomed, this Lucy may nowadays – on the occasion of a rare loan exhibition, for example – not even be able to see the objects she has come so far to see, because of the people in between; as one of the contributors to this book once remarked (on the occasion of the great Rembrandt exhibition in Amsterdam in 1956), an unfortunate result of creating an exhibition that everybody in the world wants to see can be that no one can see it – a fact demonstrated more recently to Londoners on frequent occasions in the course of the Picasso exhibition at the Tate.

But, allowing that she can see the paintings, she is likely perhaps, among all her other sufferings, to be inhibited most by a rigour of time; her days are plotted on the iron grid of a schedule.

There are of course countless other Lucies, of both sexes and all ages, as many as there are people who look at pictures. There is something of Lucy in all men and women, even in the most intelligent, the most sensitive and well informed; we are all liable, at some point or another, subconsciously to have our vision blinkered by our ability to feel what is proper, when, unlike Lucy, we have not forgotten our Baedeker, and can locate the Giottos. This book is of course made up of signposts like Baedeker, but I hope that it may do more than lay down sight-lines, which can be as lethal to works of art as lines of fire, between the spectator and each picture; that it will not impose on any over-credulous reader the belief that he is now capable of feeling what is proper in front of any of the twelve paintings here described. Sometimes indeed I feel as if the spate of words that has issued from the press, particularly since the war, is closing about art as though a cocoon were yawning wide to reclaim within its dark prison the escaped butterfly. But a virtue, it seems to me, of the intention of this series of essays is that they each point to a single object, to one painting in its physical uniqueness. Professor Talbot Rice remarks that 'the study of art is not concerned with isolated manifestations, however brilliant, but rather with a series of interlinked developments', and that is certainly a basic tenet for the art-historian. But for the individual onlooker (even if he contains an art-historian) art also manifests itself most precisely in isolated objects – in a rectangle of wood or canvas, covered with paint. The basic *experience* of a painting can only come from contemplation of the painting itself. A reproduction can tell you much; it may tell you in some cases – in an infra-red photograph, or an X-ray, for example – things that the original will not tell you, but it can never tell you precisely the same things that the original will tell your eyes. In fact one of the directions in which this book points is out of that Imaginary Museum, the Museum without Walls made famous by Malraux, out of the art books and the coloured reproductions, out of this very book, and back to the original painting.

And in front of the original painting, to stop. In front of it, to take time off. In the new age of leisure, to stop seems paradoxically to be one of the most difficult of exercises; on a Bank Holiday at the National Gallery the crowds shoal slowly past the paintings with the drifting gait of window-shoppers down Oxford Street, and it takes something moving to make us stop, to hold us quiet for half an hour: the restless shift of images on the screen of cinema or television.

I should like at this point, without becoming involved in aesthetics, to harp on the word 'beautiful'. It is significant of our time that it occurs hardly at all in the following pages; at the beginning of this century it would have spattered the pages of most writings on art fairly liberally – it enters at once into Lucy's consideration of art, in her search for the significant sepulchral slab – 'the one that was really beautiful, the one that had been most praised by Mr Ruskin'. But now it has become diminished and suspect; it begs countless questions, embarrassingly. It seems to have had relevance only so long as there was an accepted scale of values for painting, according to which paintings could be, and by some critics literally were, 'marked' according to their success in the various aspects of the art; ten marks for composition, eight for colour, but only three for drawing, and so on. In its crudest application you could use this system to assess the final value of painters, the one who scored the highest sum of marks in all aspects being the artist who produced the most beautiful pictures. Now we are, if not wiser, at least far less sure of ourselves. But still 'beauty' and 'beautiful' are words very much in current usage, if not within the specialized limits of professional circles. Often I say or think, exhausted by prevarication or by probing of qualification, that a certain picture is beautiful. I mean of course – with Mr Ayrton, as he uses the phrase in his essay – 'beautiful to me, at least'. Beauty – 'to me, at least' – in the context of pictures, relates not to an isolated quality in any painting, but to a condition in any one spectator of being aroused by a certain painting. It implies a human being resonant, in all relevant fibres of body and mind and spirit, to the impact of a work of art; interpreting it, re-creating it, as an orchestra interprets a score. But in no two people will this interpretation be the same, for no two people carry precisely the same number or quality of instruments with which to effect the interpretation. There are no proper feelings tailor-made to fit a work of art, but there is a maximum possible response of all instruments; a response that is not only an end sufficient in itself, but which enlarges the capacity of the instruments on which it registers – which is, in Berenson's famous expression, life-enhancing.

A predecessor to this account of beauty-in-action in twelve different minds was Sir Kenneth Clark's *Looking at Pictures* (1960); in that case, the reactions of one mind of remarkable sensitivity and learning to a number of masterpieces scattered throughout the great collections of Europe. The present anthology is confined to paintings visible in Great Britain, and they are not necessarily masterpieces, though all are of extraordinary quality. The process of interpretation however remains basically the same, though it is of course always extremely complex; while it may seem to be cut short the moment that you have seen the picture and passed by, it may develop and be renewed over a lifetime. To attempt to describe it and contain it in words means inevitably to simplify and to categorize the process. Sir Kenneth Clark noted in his reactions to paintings a general pattern of 'impact, scrutiny, recollection, and renewal'; he emphasizes that this is a generalization and that the texture of this pattern will vary very much, but a great many people, I imagine, will agree with the validity of this pattern as a common experience. Naturally impact comes often on first sight – what Mr Newton calls the 'peak-in-Darien' moment, in which we ask no questions. It is the moment of recognition; it may seem that, rather than your recognizing the picture, the picture has recognized you, signalling to you with authority from across the room. A picture can do this before you grasp what it represents. In the case of a contemporary painting, it may indeed have no 'story' that you can isolate. The only truly apocalyptic 'strike' of a painting on first sight that I have ever experienced was in the case of a modern picture, and I will try to describe it, even though it was a very recent painting, in a post-Cézanne language with which none of the essays in this book happens to be concerned, and even though it was so stage-managed by external conditions and a *deus ex machina* that it cannot be typical. This is however a personal anthology, and I would like, in gratitude, to record it.

The painting was by Sam Francis, a young American action painter; he would have got no marks at all from Félibien or any other critic concerned with points scored by ability in composition, drawing, etc. For action painters, as I understand them, are – or were, for they are already perhaps of the past – concerned with paint as a lover is concerned with his girl on a long summer afternoon. But a girl is of course concerned also with her lover; the engagement is mutual, and in action painting, painter and paint work one upon the other. In 1957, such paintings were still only on their way in London, and this was, I think, Francis's first one-man show in London. It was a May day, hot after rain, the sky uncomfortably scoured to an un-English blue in which monstrous cumulus clouds, loaded with darkness and armoured with blinding light, were building up for battle. It was after lunch, the traffic desultory and the air congealing in the parched and fussed Mayfair street, and I had had no lunch. I turned into Gimpel's Galleries, into the ante-room, into the narrow corridor that leads from it into the bigger room under its skylight at the back, and there on the threshold I was just aware of a huge area of white across which colour grew, putting down as it grew long delicate tendrils of colour, as a water plant puts down its roots, into the white blank of the canvas, when the lightning struck. It seemed to strike within yards, though in fact it must have been some way off, as there followed seconds of open silence, in which blindness yielded to a negative impression of the picture before me, the trailing spores pale against black, a ghost that slowly took substance again as the dazzle faded. Black dissolved to white, and across the white the colour stood; an artery of colour, red, yellow, and blue, of a structure that seemed cellular and organic, yet torn, bleeding trails of colour down into the white. These trails, that were vulgarly but the dribbles of accident, in fact stabilized the painting. It seemed, as the thunder avalanched, the most stable thing I have ever known in my life. Above the skylight, the sun was quenched, but the paint glowed as if phosphorescent, but with an extraordinary vibrant serenity, an infinite yet nervous calm that you sense sometimes in the sea at sunset. It seemed even, in that second, a painting that I could not merely live with, but almost live in, and for ever.

This was of course an unusual experience; in fact I have known nothing quite like it before or since, and later, when I read Mr

Aldous Huxley's accounts of his reactions to the drug mescalin, I seemed to recognize something that was comparable. But the essential quality is discoverable in great paintings also in moments less coincidentally heightened or concentrated by an accident of weather and mood; that quality for me is timelessness, at least the possibility of timelessness. Art today is sometimes discussed as a kind of substitute for religion for a generation that has lost faith, or indeed *as* a religion. When a painting unlocks for me that condition of timelessness, or the possibility of timelessness, its significance is I suppose closely akin to a religious one. A formal arrangement of colour and line and mass condensed within a rectangle of canvas, so many inches long and so many inches wide, can postulate infinity and eternity; no great painting is merely an anatomy of the visible world, murdered for dissection – it is a distillation of a life-force. It becomes the still centre, and its ultimate undeniable vitality remains for ever ultimately mysterious. Mystery is of course offensive to human reason but necessary for most human hearts, because in mystery there is hope, or at least the possibility of heaven or hell. So, literally often *à contre-cœur*, reason sets out to analyse, to dissect, the great works of the human imagination in paint, but happily always fails. These essays are commentaries, not dissections; words, as Mr Agnew underlines, cannot touch the heart of the matter. It cannot be said too often that great painters work in paint because there are no words for what they have to paint.

But I have got away from the first stage of the pattern of experience as outlined by Sir Kenneth Clark – impact. Impact is not necessarily on first sight. Certain painters touch one most deeply at certain stages of life and of experience; my own pattern of love-affairs with painters – as with writers – seems entirely irrational. My first love in adolescence was Van Gogh, almost simultaneously with a more stable one with Holbein. Then there were the Impressionists, and much later Cézanne coupled with Raphael. With Poussin I had a long-delayed reaction; for years I had looked at Poussins with desire and admiration: I knew where he stood, what he stood for – like Lucy, I knew myself to be excellently equipped for feeling what was proper – but only in 1960, at the Louvre Poussin exhibition, did Poussin click for me. Other painters have taken me by surprise, crept up on me as it were without my being aware of it; both Turner and Corot did that, and so did Courbet. Sometimes the obvious has revealed itself in abrupt splendour, very late; thus I went into the chapel at Padua, rather cross, knowing what I was going to see and already bored by it, and a few moments later my soul was levitating with Giotto in corporeal majesty. Later I told someone that I had discovered Giotto, and he looked at me with a tolerant sneer; but he was wrong, because I *had* discovered Giotto. Some painters still remain locked against me – most of Rubens (though not all), the big 'machines' bruise me; the now-fashionable Italian *seicento*, except Salvator Rosa and Strozzi, with both of whom I had passionate early attachments; unlike Mr Newton, I cannot go with Tintoretto, or only rarely, and when I think of the Scuola di San Rocco I remember, willy-nilly, mainly a crick in the neck. To only two painters, I think, have I remained unswervingly loyal for all the years I have looked at paintings seriously; both Dutchmen, Rembrandt and Vermeer, steady as unwinking lighthouses, those twin polarities of the human spirit. But over the years I have grown more patient, and am content now to wait; either I shall know one day what the painters are about whom I do not register, or I shall not. It is more dangerous to wait in the case of paintings than of books, because of the place-factor. I seem for example to be congenitally allergic to Henry James as a novelist, but any day anywhere I may pick up a book of his and discover how wrong I was; but if, when I go to New York, the impression which I have always had from reproductions that *Guernica* is a major catastrophe in the work of Picasso seems to be confirmed by my eyes in front of the original, I may never be in New York again to correct or re-confirm that impression.

The second and third phases in contemplation of painting are scrutiny and recollection, and it is with these that the following pages are most concerned. Scrutiny is the close reading to confirm that you saw what you thought you saw: the exploration of the whole terrain, of its interlinked felicities of detail and their modulation into the whole; the story-matter of the picture. (In my own case, I find my mind gropes for this even in abstracts; images begin to cohere, a landscape or a face seems about to unveil from unimaged colour, and then dissolve again, but leaving the form and colour the richer – I have been rebuked by an abstract painter when I admitted this, but that is the way it works for me.) The third stage, recollection, proceeds simultaneously as the painting places itself within a framework of knowledge, within a certain period of time, within a certain geographical school of painting, within a certain trend of style, and within the work of a certain painter. Distinctions of quality formulate themselves, often modifying very sharply the judgement of the first impact; the tension slackens – this may be a copy, and you realize that what you thought you saw was its archetype, an original somewhere else, and that you were wrong. Or delight in pure skill may surface, or concern at condition, the nag of doubt as to the relationship between what you now see and what the painter originally left as finished on his canvas: what he intended you to see.

It may not be improper for me to say a little about condition at this point, as the centuries-old controversy about cleaning has been rampant since the war, and distinguished advocates of the two most important points of view are contributors to this book. The ideal condition for any painting is of course *mint*: that is, as the artist left it, with all accretions of discolouring and therefore distorting dirt and old yellowed varnish scrupulously removed from the surface without disturbing the original paint. Unfortunately, this ideal condition is strictly ideal and never to be consummated, for all paintings begin to change the moment they are finished; through the years, they settle into their support and the very structure of the paint shifts. The colour alters; in a humid climate such as that of England, particularly if the painting is on wood, the paint and its support shrink and swell at different speeds, and inevitably the adhesion of one to the other is weakened and the picture begins to flake. The surface is vulnerable to all the hazards of daily life, to bruising, to abrasion, to centuries of dusting; in the past it was vulnerable to the attentions of cleaners and restorers less expert than are those of today and more lavish in their repaint. It is subject to the fluctuations of taste – a drapery may be painted on to a nude here or a skull removed from a still-life there. The surface of an old picture in a raking light can look like a battlefield pitted and scored by the havoc of time. The re-presentation of the original surface can in almost all cases therefore be an approximation only. This is now recognized by all responsible people, and controversy tends to centre on two main points: that some of the original paint – usually the very thin final glazes of colour that painters used to modulate their pictures into tonal coherence – is in fact being destroyed by the cleaners; or that, if these glazes no longer exist, owing to earlier damage, or have changed colour so that they no longer fulfil their intended purpose (as they do inevitably if they were originally mixed with varnish which turns yellow), then the accretions of time should not be 'stripped to the bone' but only to that point which suits the individual painting best. Both these questions are open to argument that can never be conclusive, unless some demonstrable mistake exists. The only person who can really know whether original paint has been removed is often the restorer himself, but it is almost impossible in most cases to prove to the satisfaction of any second party that he has not done so. The other question, as to how far cleaning should be taken, comes down in the end to a matter of individual eye and judgement, a matter again of taste. The controversy is however a very healthy one from one point of view, as it bears witness to the continuance of an informed and passionately aware body of public opinion, which is very salutary for those whose duty it is to conserve great paintings that belong to the nation; as a professional curator myself, I know the value of this controversy both as sheer nuisance-value and as furthering a continual extension of knowledge and of alertness.

But the other point I would like to underline is the fascinating and almost miraculous stamina of great paintings. I have heard it said for example of the startling blues in the cleaned Titians at the National

Gallery that now almost bombard the spectator, that if that was what Titian meant he was a bad painter. But what continues to amaze me about the Titians – apart from the question whether the blues should be toned down so that they 'read' tonally with the rest of the picture as a whole, or not – is the enduring vitality of the images, their refusal to be wrecked, the majestic authority that still carries through what ought logically to be the dissolution of its component parts into nonsense. This is partly because one makes mental adjustments as a matter of course – we do not see with the naked eye, and anyone who believes in the concept of the 'innocent' eye would do well to read Professor Gombrich's *Art and Illusion*. But, for me, the Titians still remain potent to arouse beauty, just as do the battered Mantegnas at Hampton Court which Mr Robertson discusses.

The awareness of the condition of a painting is but part of the processes of scrutiny and recollection; the responses to this process are those of the gamut available within each onlooker, and will be the more richly complex (though not necessarily the sharper) the more richly complex that gamut is; the individual sensibility strung and tuned by knowledge and experience. Knowledge of course brings also its casualties; much in the following essays is concerned with siting a painting within the context of its time, and such knowledge is drastically winnowing in action. Thus, as one gets to know more about a period and a school of painting, one finds that a picture that once seemed very exciting is to be seen entirely conditioned by its period – simply a period piece. Then one realizes that it is purely derivative, and it sinks almost without trace into its period. The positive action of knowledge and experience is not only to shed light on a great painting, to enlarge one's comprehension of it, but also to clear the ground about it so that one can see it emerge alive from the dead past. It refuses finally to be conditioned by the prison of its time, but is formidably of our own and of all time. And that, I suppose, is the close of the cycle of apprehension, the renewal which is another beginning. A renewal in each individual through a lifetime perhaps, a reinterpretation by each succeeding generation, a rediscovery of the core of vitality that persists in every great work of art and endures against time.

Towards the close of *A Room with a View*, Lucy, having suffered much but won through, expresses her debt to that forthright character, old Mr Emerson. 'It was as if he had made her see the whole of everything at once.' I would not of course begin to suggest that this book could bring about such a condition in its reader; nor would I claim personally that any picture has ever brought about in myself a consummation so exalted and so appalling. One cannot even see the whole of any one picture at once, let alone everything. But I do know that in some paintings, in the heart of their live stillness, I have been convinced that it at least might be possible to see the whole of everything at once: that 'everything' might form a whole.

David Piper

Enjoying Paintings

The Water Carrier

Velázquez

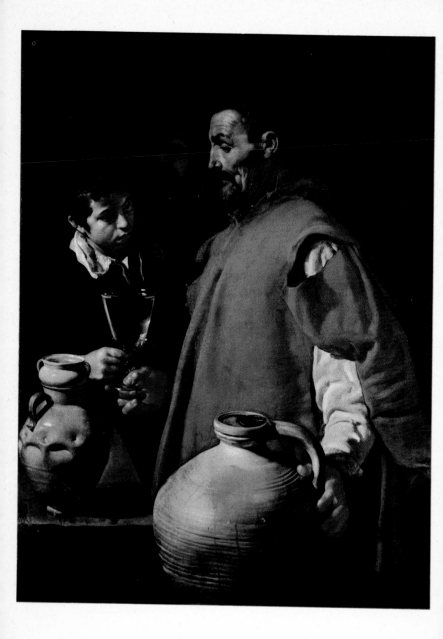

No artist, I think, is more difficult to analyse in the spoken or written word than the great Spaniard, Velázquez. Virginia Woolf once posed the dilemma of all art critics before such a painter's painter. It is after dinner and the talk has fallen on painting:

Now they are going into the silent land. Soon they will be out of reach of the human voice. They are making passes with their hands to express what they cannot say. What excites them is something so deeply sunk that they cannot put words to it.

Nevertheless passes with the hands are not enough: words must somehow be found.

The difficulty is that Velázquez himself does not give us much help. No artist conceals himself more successfully behind his pictures. He shares with Piero della Francesca the distinction of being the most impersonal of artists. We know the facts of his uneventful life; his youth in Seville; his subsequent life in Madrid as court painter to Philip IV, broken only by his two journeys to Italy. We know something of his independence, his dignity, the serenity of his character, the modesty which so impressed Rubens, and his self-confidence. But of what he felt we know little, for he painted without ever betraying an emotion.

Some such impersonality in method is, I suspect, a condition of all great art. Emotion must be recalled in tranquillity; the artist is more concerned with what arouses emotion than with the emotion itself. But what Mr Berenson wrote of Piero della Francesca is equally true of Velázquez. He loved impersonality, the absence of expressed emotion, as a quality in itself. Such impersonality forces us back, when we try to analyse a picture by Velázquez, to the purely artistic qualities of form and design, colour and tone values. It also impresses us with a heroic quality, placing the artist above the level of ordinary mankind.

At first sight, however, there is nothing especially heroic about the

1. Velázquez: *Old Woman Cooking Eggs*, c. 1618. The National Gallery of Scotland, Edinburgh

subject of the picture I have chosen here: Velázquez's *The Water Carrier* at Apsley House in London. Palomino, the biographer of Velázquez, writing in 1724, described it as a picture 'in which is seen a poorly dressed old man, clad in a coarse and ragged jacket, giving drink to an urchin'. Add the head of a second boy in the background, a glass, a table, a jug, and a large earthenware jar, and you have the entire ingredients. The picture was painted in Seville,

Velázquez's home town, about 1618, when the artist was nineteen years old. It required considerable independence to choose such a subject from everyday life in a country where religion was the proper theme for an artist. No doubt Velázquez was influenced by the celebrated picaresque stories of his contemporary Cervantes, and by the example of realistic painting set by Caravaggio. *The Water Carrier* is one of a small group of pictures called *bodegones*, familiar scenes of life in kitchen or tavern with a prominent accompaniment of still life. They were painted by Velázquez at the start of his career. There is another, *The Two Boys at a Table*, also in Apsley House; and *Old Woman Cooking Eggs*, at Edinburgh [1], is of the same type and approximately the same date.

Fine though the Edinburgh picture is, *The Water Carrier* is, for my taste, by far the most beautiful of all Velázquez's early pictures, out-topping even the wonderful *Adoration of the Kings* in the Prado [2]. There is, indeed, something mysterious in the way *The Water Carrier* outstrips in profundity and accomplishment all the other pictures which we know of this period. Certainly that was the opinion of Velázquez's contemporaries. It was the picture Velázquez took to Madrid in 1623 to show to Philip and Olivares as a sample of his skill. It was hung by the King in his palace. It was named by Palomino 'as among the most esteemed works of the artist'. It was particularly admired by Raphael Mengs, that rather dull painter but shrewd judge of pictures, to whom the rediscovery of Velázquez in the eighteenth century was principally due.

'The best models of the natural style are the works of Diego Velázquez' – so wrote Mengs. It was this naturalism, this realistic representation of the thing seen, which to many of his admirers was Velázquez's greatest quality. Pacheco, under whom Velázquez studied and who, as his friend and father-in-law, accompanied him to Madrid, had taught: 'I hold to the principle that Nature ought to be the chief master.' It was a principle with which Velázquez was much in sympathy. Throughout his life he relied on and painted from the model. His pictures came to him through the eye rather than through the imagination.

2. Velázquez: *The Adoration of the Kings, c.* 1619. The Prado, Madrid

The chief figure in *The Water Carrier* was an old Corsican, whose occupation was watering the streets of Seville and who, in return, had the right to supply water to the houses in the town. The boy to whom he is handing the glass was a studio boy whom Velázquez often paid to sit for him and who occurs in several other pictures. *The Water Carrier* was evidently painted in the studio. From the acute angle at which the light strikes the figures, as it does also in the *Old Woman Cooking Eggs*, the source of light must have been a window high in the wall; from the narrowness of the shaft of light the window was probably small, the wall thick. Not only the forceful lighting with its vigorous chiaroscuro, but also the heads, the clothes, and the still life are depicted with perfect naturalism.

The draughtsmanship is masterly. Drawing seems to have come naturally to Velázquez at an early age. You have only to examine the hands (somewhat plump, with tapering fingers, as always with Velázquez) or the eye sockets to assure yourself of that. The Corsican is represented as a dignified old man and seen with searching intimacy. The boy holds his pose with ease. His head owes something to El Greco, his look is concentrated, eager, attentive. Whether painting kings or dwarfs or more ordinary human beings, Velázquez always thoroughly understood the art of characterization. Unlike his contemporary Van Dyck, Velázquez, in his portraits, always puts the personality of the sitter first, his own style as a painter second. And the still life in the foreground is painted as are the living people. The picture has a certain Spanish austerity and great sincerity. Compared with another, avowedly realistic picture, Rembrandt's *The Anatomy Lesson*, also the work of a young man, *The Water Carrier* is far more successfully unified and far more alive. It is one of the astonishing facts about *The Water Carrier* that a picture which is so immensely still (and Velázquez was seldom a painter of action) should convey so much feeling of life.

I have described *The Water Carrier* so far as one might describe a picture painted by a highly gifted Flemish realist. But naturalism, the painting of appearances only – so horribly like, as Cézanne used to complain – is of course not enough. 'Truly art lies hid in nature, he has her that can draw her out.' Dürer meant indeed much the same as Cézanne: 'If only I could realize'; if it was only possible to paint the reality behind the appearance, the fundamental and less transitory nature of the object, the essence, so to speak; if it was only possible to discover beneath appearances some underlying structural unity. In pursuit of that ideal, every picture for Cézanne and for Velázquez became a fresh effort of realizing and expressing what they judged was significant.

If significance, then, not pure verisimilitude, was Velázquez's aim, it became necessary, consciously or unconsciously, to plan, to arrange, above all to simplify. The design of *The Water Carrier* is highly deliberate. We know that for Velázquez the shape of the canvas was very important. He sometimes sewed on extra strips to obtain the exact proportions which satisfied him. *The Water Carrier* may have lost an inch or so round the edges when cut from its stretchers by Joseph Bonaparte on his flight from Madrid. (It was packed, together with 164 other unframed pictures, in the carriage captured by the Tenth Hussars after the Battle of Vittoria.) But the figures must always have been narrowly confined within the space and this concentration gives great weight and power. The three closely knit heads are balanced by the glass, the jug, and the jar, which in shape and emphasis echo the figures themselves. In one sense the living people are treated like still life. In another sense the still life acquires something of the character of the figures. The light strikes diagonally across the boy's cheek and collar, falling fiercely on the white of the old man's sleeve. The glass collects and concentrates the light at the nodal point of the picture.

The counterpoint of uprights and diagonals, triangles and ovals is extremely elaborate. The most important unseen lines seem to me to be those that drop plumb from the old man's cheek-bone to the centre of the jar and from the boy's left cheek-bone to the centre of the glass. The design is also very much in depth, from the great jar in the foreground to the half-seen head at the back. This third head, and the shadows against which the group is posed, have to some extent deadened and sunk into the preparatory ground. Nevertheless a great corridor of space drives back between the old man and the jar on one side, the two boys and the glass on the other. This corridor is bridged by the two hands which unite the design both in depth and in the flat, and something of the same function is performed by the long sweep of the old man's arm culminating in the curves of the jar.

The colour of *The Water Carrier* is in itself not very remarkable. It is somewhat parchment-like – perhaps a reflection of the coloured earths of Seville. But it is in the absolute harmony of colour rather than in any brilliance of individual colouring that the grand effect resides. Browns and olives, blacks and whites give a dignity and solemnity to the whole scene. This harmony is built up by the modifications caused in colour by light, by the relation and gradation of tones within the colours. No artist had a surer sense of tone values than Velázquez. By those tones he expressed both form and space. The amplitude of form, the mighty roundness of the earthenware jar, is created by an infinite variety and range of tones. What a texture those tones make on the ringed surface of the jar! Isolate the still life and you have pure Chardin. The head of the boy is delicately shaped by the broken lights and shadows on the face, by the range of warm tones in the hair, and by the contrasting cool tones in the collar. You can see by comparison how Caravaggio, in the Louvre picture, achieved the same effect with his boy's head, but he has used the lighting with less subtlety than Velázquez and with more dramatic intention.

In the dress of the old man Velázquez has built up, on brown undertones, such a complex orchestration of yellows and browns and reds, and has contrasted it so boldly with the intense white of the sleeve, that he has deliberately had to flatten the figure by hardening the folds of the drapery and emphasizing the contour. Otherwise the form would have become too dominant. This creation of forms by tones looks so easy, as when Canaletto gives the very substance of a wall by playing with the variations made on it by light. It is in fact one of the most difficult artistic achievements, requiring an absolute certainty of eye and hand; and all great artists who have an intense feeling for form, Leonardo, Degas, Rembrandt, Velázquez, do their modelling in this way.

The Water Carrier is therefore far from being a purely naturalistic scene, a realistic rendering or glimpse of some everyday incident in the lives of simple people. It is based on a complex architectural design, with more than a hint of mathematics in its structure. All insignificant detail, such as you would find in real life, has been simplified away in the attempt to give only the essentials of what is portrayed. The old man has become as impersonal as a god, or as his earthenware jar, the symbol of detachment from life. And wood has never been so wooden as in that long-enduring table. Finally, light in its effect on colour has become one of the participants in the picture, creating the forms on which it plays. 'Truly art lies hid in Nature': Velázquez has drawn her out. In doing so he has fixed the old man, his two boys, his studio properties, in a permanent relationship. How he has managed, through a glass and the hands that meet over the stem [3], to create such a mysterious feeling of tension between his old man and his boy, a sense that they share a secret, that the passing of a glass of water is to them an act of intense significance, I simply do not know. Cézanne, out of peasants playing cards at the inn, constructed a monumental composition in which everything, even the pipes on the wall, has a significance greater than life [4]. Velázquez, out of equally ordinary material, created, by his feeling for and ability to realize form, 'an epic scene, in which gestures and events take on a Homeric ease and amplitude' – and with the glass playing the part of Cézanne's pipes. There is something of the sense of proportion of a Greek temple or Greek sculpture in the grave rhythms of *The Water Carrier*, the combination of a broad majestic beauty of effect with perfection of finish.

Later in his life Velázquez was to become a more creative, an even more original, artist. He developed a greater feeling for space, a feeling which reached its height in *The Ladies-in-Waiting* and *The Tapestry Weavers* in the Prado. He became more of a colourist, as in the *Portrait of Philip IV in the Country at Fraga*, now in the Frick Collection, New York. The impressionistic technique, with which he learnt to lay his tones against each other, made him one of the founders of modern art. The brilliant and faithful heir of Caravaggio

3. Detail from *The Water Carrier*

4. Cézanne: *The Card Players, c.* 1890–92. Stephen C. Clark Collection, New York

became the hero of Whistler. His visits to Italy and the influence of Venetian painting in particular enriched his palette and broadened his handling. 'Raphael, to be plain with you,' he said to Salvator Rosa, 'for I like to be candid and outspoken, does not please me at all. In Venice are found the good and the beautiful; to their brush I give the first place; it is Titian that bears the banner.'

But, although *The Water Carrier* does not represent all of Veláz-quez, I find in its austerely formal qualities a completely satisfying picture and a forerunner of that superb achievement the *Portrait of*

Innocent X in Rome, with which it shares the same inevitability of pose. 'Not painted but willed on to the canvas,' said Mengs. '*Non pintura ma verdad*', not painting but the truth. I do not think that is an exaggerated description of this, the first of Velázquez's masterpieces. But now, if I go further, I shall go into the silent land and start making passes with my hands. So I must leave you to study for yourselves Velázquez's *Water Carrier of Seville*. Thanks to the fortunes of war and to the great generosity of the present Duke of Wellington, it now belongs to the nation.

*

Biographical note

Diego Rodriguez de Silva y Velázquez was born in Seville in 1599. Except for continuous difficulties in obtaining payment from his royal patron Philip IV, the artist's life was happy and uncomplicated; by nature he was serene and confident; and his art developed steadily and with an ever-increasing concentration and simplicity. His teacher from an early age was Francisco Pacheco, a man of learning and sympathy, a connoisseur and a competent painter who from the start recognized his pupil's genius. In 1618, after five years in Pacheco's studio, Velázquez married his daughter and maintained with his father-in-law a lifelong friendship. Velázquez's style in the early days in Seville was based on the realism which Caravaggio had introduced into painting in Italy [5]. It is unlikely that at that time Velázquez had ever seen an original by Caravaggio; but the feeling for the Caravaggesque was in the air and pervaded all painting in the early seventeenth century. In this period he is at his most naturalistic, using strong chiaroscuro in the modelling, with yellowish-brown flesh tints, and aiming at simple, powerful effects.

By 1623 Velázquez, his wife, and his father-in-law had settled in Madrid. At the suggestion of the Conde Duque de Olivares, Philip IV's favourite and chief minister, Velázquez was commissioned to paint the first of many portraits of the King. In the same year he was appointed painter to the Royal Family, in whose service he remained

37

5. Caravaggio: *Portrait of Olaf de Wigancourt, c.* 1601. The Louvre, Paris

for the rest of his life. The portrait of the King's brother, the Infante Don Carlos [6], dates from some three years after the painter's arrival in Madrid. During these first six years in Madrid Velázquez's style retained much of its Sevillian character, but there was greater simplicity of treatment, less interest in detail, and more transparency in the shadows. In 1628 Rubens visited Madrid, and Velázquez was instructed by the King to act as his guide and host. Together the two great painters visited the Escorial and, from the mountainside, sketched the scene below. No doubt it was Rubens who inspired Velázquez with the wish to visit Italy. With the King's permission he set out in 1629 for a tour of some eighteen months, during which time he visited Venice, Rome, and Naples. The journey to Italy lightened and made more brilliant Velázquez's colour and the shadows became still more transparent.

The eighteen years between Velázquez's first and second visits to Italy were the most prolific of his career. His handling became freer and his style, from the forties onwards, was almost what we now call impressionistic. The great series of Royal portraits in the Prado and the well-known *Surrender of Breda* date from this period. During Velázquez's second visit to Italy, from 1649 to 1651, he painted little except the magnificent portrait of the Pope Innocent X.

During the last nine years of his life he was more and more concerned with official duties; but *Las Meninas* (The Ladies-in-Waiting) and *Las Hilanderas* (The Tapestry Weavers), both in the Prado, are two of his greatest achievements. On 31 July 1660 he was struck by fever, and he died in Madrid on 6 August.

History of *The Water Carrier*

The Water Carrier was the picture which gained Velázquez most fame before he left his home town. Seville was the exclusive port for trade with the New World and for the sailings of the Silver Fleet and therefore attracted many foreigners. It was laid out with many parks and gardens, and the watering of the dusty ground was the duty of a special guild of *aguadores* under the control of an *alguacil* or constable. Many of these water sprinklers were Frenchmen and among them was a certain Corsican, a popular character of the town, whom Velázquez used for his model as the principal figure in *The Water Carrier*. Of the two other figures, the boy with the glass appears again in the *Old Woman Cooking Eggs* [1], and the boy drinking may well be the same model used in the *Two Young Men at a Table*, also at Apsley House. In *The Adoration of the Kings* [2] the king on the left bears a striking resemblance to the Corsican.

Francisco Pacheco in describing these early pictures of Velázquez wrote that *bodegones*

are certainly to be valued, that is when painted as Velázquez paints them, for in this branch he has attained such an eminence that he has left room for no rival. They deserve high esteem; for with these elements and with portraiture he discovered the true imitation of Nature and encouraged many by his powerful example.... He kept an apprentice lad, who for payment served him as a model in various attitudes and postures, weeping, laughing, in all imaginable difficult parts. After this model he drew many heads in charcoal and chalk on blue paper and made many similar studies after many other natives, thereby acquiring a sure hand in hitting off likenesses.

These drawings have disappeared, but we can follow the history of *The Water Carrier* to the present day. It is described by the painter Antonio Palomino in his *Museo Pictorico*, published in the early eighteenth century, from which comes much of our knowledge of the details of Velázquez's life. It was chosen to hang in one of the apartments in the Palace of Buen Retiro in Madrid, where it is recorded in 1700 as *El Corzo, aguador*. Later it passed to the new Bourbon Palace, where it was seen in 1755 in the 'Serenade Hall' by the Italian Caimo, together with many other pictures by Velázquez. It was certainly highly prized by Joseph Bonaparte, who had been placed on the throne of Spain by Napoleon, for, at the time of his flight from Madrid in 1813, it was one of the many treasures which he carried away. After his defeat by the Duke of Wellington at the Battle of Vittoria his pictures were captured with his baggage.

6. Velázquez: *The Infante Don Carlos, c.* 1625–6. The Prado, Madrid

Characteristically, Wellington offered to return them. The Spanish Ambassador in London informed the Duke, however, that King Ferdinand VII, now restored to the throne, 'touched by your delicacy does not wish to deprive you of that which has come into your possession by means as just as they are honourable'. Thus they remained in the possession of the Wellington family until 1947.

Two other versions of *The Water Carrier* are known to exist. The first, in which the Corsican wears a rough cap, is possibly from Velázquez's own hand, although weaker than the Apsley House version. It is in the collection of the late Count Contini-Bonaccossi in Florence. The other, which is clearly a studio version of the Contini picture, is in the Walters Gallery, Baltimore, U.S.A.

Books for reference

Allende-Salazar, Juan, *Velazquez*, Stuttgart, 1925

Armstrong, Sir Walter, *Velazquez: a study of his life and art*, 1896

Beruete, A. de, *Velázquez*, 1906

Curtis, Charles B., *Velazquez and Murillo*, 1883

Fargue, Léon-Paul, *Velazquez*, Paris, 1946

Ford, Richard, *Handbook for Travellers in Spain*, two vols., 1845

Justi, Carl, *Diego Velazquez and his times*, 1889

Mayer, August L., *Velazquez: a catalogue raisonné*, 1936

Palomino de Castro y Velasco, A. Antonio, *El Museo Pictorico*, 1724

Stevenson, R.A.M., *Velasquez*, 1899

Stirling-Maxwell, Sir William, *Velazquez and his Works*, 1855

The Music Party

Watteau

The Music Party hangs in a room at the Wallace Collection which contains seven paintings by Watteau – and it must be about the only room in England which does. Two other large ones hang in a room near by.

As a picture it is by no means Watteau's greatest achievement. It is not so beautiful – to me, at least – as two other little panels in the same gallery, the *Harlequin and Columbine* and the small version of the *Champs-Élysées*; nor is it so perfect as the painting at Dulwich; nor does it compare with the *Gilles* in the Louvre; nor does it approach for one moment the supreme, the last, the incomparable *L'Enseigne de Gersaint*, that shop sign for a picture dealer, which is now in Berlin. Yet *The Music Party* has Watteau's special magic, and it is because this magic is present in all his works in all circumstances, because he could not touch a crayon to paper, nor a brush – even a dirty brush – to canvas, without creating a fragment of unique and mysterious quality, that I have chosen to discuss it here. It displays his faults, and his debts to Rubens and the Venetians. It even contains an unusual, an amazing, piece of clumsiness, totally unlike him in its imperfection.

But if you look at it where it hangs with the work of his immediate followers – with paintings extraordinarily similar in subject and treatment by Pater and Lancret; with paintings by subsequent generations who also owed their vision to him – then even the admirable and accomplished pictures of Boucher fade into insignificance in Watteau's company; even the masterpieces of Fragonard. When you leave the room, it is Watteau who leaves it with you, Watteau who haunts you.

The Music Party is typical Watteau in its choice of subject, the disposition of the figures, the limpid delicacy of its landscape. His world was a stage peopled by aristocrats who have no pressing problems: by ladies to whom the whispered compliment is all and gentlemen who turn a phrase and execute a gesture with studied elegance. Yet they are melancholy. When they sing one can almost hear with what subtle phrasing the gentlemen blend their light tenor voices with the soft mezzo-soprani of the ladies. The songs are by Lully: the voices would not be adequate for opera. They have no cares, these people, yet they are melancholy. They are always in the garden, but the day is never hot. Their love is formal, their lust a matter of prestige.

Why, then, are those puppets so moving? They are butterflies. One can well understand why, less than a century later, the stern puritans who followed Jacques-Louis David, the great artist of the French Revolution, should have brushed them aside, and why David's pupils should have flicked bread pellets – bread pellets black with charcoal from rubbing at their nobly wooden drawings – at the Watteau which hung in their life class. And that painting was *L'Embarquement pour l'Île de Cythère*, depicting a party of young people taking ship for the island of love. This was his diploma picture – and the first to be called a *fête galante*.

But to see the participants in Watteau's pictures as ghosts is to be too hasty. Slight and inconsequential though their activities may be, feckless as they may seem, they have bones and flesh and blood. The strength of their forms, beneath the rustling silks, is by no means insubstantial. Watteau was after all a Fleming, for all his Parisian delicacy, and a trace of that robust race is always apparent in the drawing of his figures. Furthermore, Watteau's debt to Rubens is so strong that the same blood seems to run in their veins, even though in Watteau it was thinned by the ravages of consumption.

The Goncourts say that Rubens 'wanders a stranger through Watteau's *fêtes champêtres* where the tumult of the senses has been stilled', and certainly the earthy richness of Rubens, although he 'lives on in [Watteau's] palette of carmine and golden flesh tints', is not at first apparent in Watteau's painting. His colour, often silvered by his love for Veronese's cooler range, is lunar where Rubens's echoes the full blaze of sun. The fat rollick of Rubens's dancing peasants, the vigorous activities of his robust divinities, is transmuted to the elegant posturing of slender members of the smart set. But without the warm example and noble repose of Rubens's *Garden of Love* the amorous conduct of Watteau's *fêtes champêtres* might have been differently conceived.

Watteau was one of those artists naturally given to nostalgia. To him, one suspects, a golden age – an age of Rubens, of Titian's *Bacchanals*, of the fiery loves of gods with mortals – lived on as in a dream, silver, not golden.

> *Dans le vieux parc solitaire et glacé*
> *Deux spectres ont évoqué le passé,*

as Paul Verlaine, re-evoking Watteau in his turn, saw and celebrated the silver age, then passed.

Yet they are not spectres. The fingers, taut and bony, with which Mezzetin tunes his lute in the centre of *The Music Party* are vital and full of strength, but a sinewy, not a weighty strength. Look at the hands in Watteau's drawings and paintings and their muscularity is as astonishing as their delicacy. They clamp the lute strings, where Rubens wrapped them round a sword hilt; but could Watteau's gentlemen not have held a rapier, if necessary?

Watteau chose the *fête champêtre*, or *fête galante* as it came to be called in his work, as the setting for his elegants. It has a long tradition. This glade, this gently disordered garden which you can see peopled by graceful personages through the colonnade in *The Music Party*, was once the home of pagan gods. Bellini, looking back to a dream of Parnassus, had the gods picnic there, and Titian got them drunk. Rubens got them drunker; Poussin calmed them in the evening. In such a place Giorgione was at home. On Greek islands now bare and washed as the seashore, such as Andros and Naxos, the gods had trifled with privileged mortals, and their stories, conjured by Philostratus, had sent the painters of Venice into a dream of wine and golden glory, 2,000 years later.

Watteau took this place – this dream landscape – and peopled it with the gentry. He took the details of the landscape itself from the Luxembourg Gardens and made an Elysium of the Champs-Élysées and peopled it, not with gods, but with gallants. But who are these idle persons? They are not the courtiers of Versailles, all pomp and protocol. They are not the vagabonds of the theatre, whose costumes they often wear, and in whom Watteau's master, Claude Gillot, took such saturnine pleasure. They are a poet's figments, a concourse *en travesti*, dressed sometimes in the costumes of the ball, sometimes as Pierrot, Harlequin, Scapin, Tartaglia, Gilles, and Mezzetin. And even these rakish puppets trace their ancestry, in the *commedia dell'arte*, to the Atellan fables of ancient Rome. Puppets with a lineage, they refine their bawdy jokes for ladies' ears, but the gossip is still a scandal.

What is important – what saves Watteau from *fin de siècle longueurs* – is that vitality and precision which, however broken in health he himself was (and he was slowly dying of tuberculosis in all the latter part of his life), he imparted to his figures in painting and above all in drawing. He avoided sentimentality by the sheer penetration of his glance. He was a matchless observer of living people and a great natural draughtsman.

There is a study in chalks by Watteau of three seated women [7]. One of them reaches across her guitar, her shoulder as tense as steel under the satin. Her hand is not in sight yet her fingers pluck the strings with sharp accuracy, and you can feel this from the action of her arm. The turned head is vigorously concentrated, crisply modelled, as sharply cut as a cameo. In *The Music Party* to which she has been transferred, she is softer, and this brings us to the sad fact that, great though he was, Watteau's temperament all too frequently betrayed him in the execution of a painting. The drawings are incomparable, the painting is seldom quite so fresh, quite so crisp.

He was impatient – so impatient that his friend and biographer Le Comte de Caylus criticized him most sternly for it. In his love for rapidity of effect – and he worked at fantastic speed – he made no proper preparation for a picture. He would select from his sketchbooks a group of drawings and transpose them to canvas [8]. All the main figures in *The Music Party* exist as separate drawings [7, 9, 10] made at different times, except, by chance, that of the central figure with a lute, which has been lost (although an engraving of it does exist).

7. Watteau: Studies of three seated women (two of them playing the guitar); black and red chalks. The Louvre, Paris

Having selected a group he would paint *du premier coup*, using thick paint, and if he wished to correct a passage he would rub it away with an oily rag and paint again at once. He rarely cleaned his palette and, according to Caylus, the pot of thick oil he used was 'full of dirt and dust, and mixed with all sorts of colours which adhered to his brushes'. The result was the eventual ruin sometimes of whole pictures, sometimes of parts of them. In *The Music Party* the lady with her hands folded in the left-hand group is badly

8. Detail from *The Music Party*, to illustrate Watteau's method of assembling un-related drawings into a composition. Such drawings were not made as preparatory studies for any specific painting, but were selected from sketchbooks and incorporated, with minor modifications, as occasion arose. The standing figure of Gilles has been identified as a portrait of Nicholas Wleughels

discoloured, and the Negro page on the right is clotted and messy, especially his head and left hand. A further maladroitness and an astonishing one is the hand of the figure of Gilles on the extreme left of the group. In the drawing for it [9] the hand lies loosely on the chair-back, faultlessly drawn. In the painting it is hastily and horribly botched – ill-articulated, deformed even – so badly indeed that one might charitably hope it is the work of a restorer. But I fear it is not. In many of Watteau's finest pictures one may find this kind of deterioration, this small hint of carelessness.

Watteau's exclusive use of existing drawings was unusual. Most artists of his time made specific preparatory drawings for their different pictures. Rubens, for instance – Watteau's great forerunner – has left hundreds of composition studies and detailed drawings from models, clearly made with specific pictures in mind. True, he would sometimes insert a figure from an earlier picture of his own, or even sometimes a figure from another artist's work, but in general he would plan a new composition with the care of a general launching an attack. When his plan of campaign was fully envisaged his army of assistants would put the prepared plan into action, transfering the drawings to canvas. Rubens might then make drastic alterations in completing the picture, but his forces had been carefully disposed. This careful practice was usual but not invariable. Poussin, although so deliberate and classical a master, seems to have found such preliminary notation largely unnecessary; so did Rembrandt. Their drawings are mostly shorthand notes, however marvellous, and as for Velázquez, since only a handful of drawings of any kind exist by him, it may be that he did the whole job direct on the canvas. Yet Watteau's method is still unusual.

As for his painting, the faults are these. Until the nineteenth century paintings were built up in layers and paint was applied thinly, especially in the dark areas of the canvas. Even Rembrandt limited his heavy impasto to his lights, and if he over-painted these it was with the thinnest of transparent glazes. This is because it is vital that a passage of oil paint be dry before it is over-painted. By scrubbing out with oil and painting again immediately on the resulting wet surface, Watteau endangered the permanence of his pictures because paint contracts as it dries and different stages of drying contract at different speeds. Wet paint on partially dry paint leads to clotting, wrinkling, and finally cracking, and much twentieth-century painting will die of it. Manipulating this sticky mass is what Sickert used to call 'mauling the paint', and although it is extraordinary to imagine an artist of Watteau's extreme delicacy of touch mauling his paint, that is what from time to time he did.

But Watteau was an artist working against time, and he was, according to Caylus, at once listless and lazy, yet given to a vivacity which inspired in him 'an eager need to transfer at once to canvas some effect conceived in the imagination'. He was, we are told, morose and caustic, timid, ill-favoured, restless, capricious, unstable, and of a temperament *sombre et mélancolique* – unhappy qualities some of which may be the symptoms of consumption. We are also told he could produce such drawings as are contained in the magnificent collection of his studies in the British Museum at a rate of one an hour, working in his favourite drawing medium of three chalks – black, white, and sanguine red – on tinted paper. Small wonder, perhaps that such virtuosity tempted him to careless rapidity in painting. We are the losers.

Ill-favoured and graceless, Antoine Watteau restored grace to French art after a pompous century of grandiose painting. His greatest French predecessor, Nicolas Poussin, had promoted this tendency in his followers, for Poussin is the noblest of French classical artists, and noble classicism in the hands of those who do not understand it, and cannot encompass it, leads to empty rhetoric. From Watteau stemmed the whole art of the eighteenth century in France, with the one outstanding exception of Chardin, and, despite the wonderful gifts of Fragonard, most of Watteau's followers were as frivolous and trivial as Poussin's were pompous and rhetorical. In the seventeen-nineties Poussin came back into his own and Watteau was eclipsed by the neo-classicists, of whom David and Ingres were the greatest. Watteau was again restored to favour, strangely enough, in no small measure because of Ingres. It is in this

9. Watteau: *Nicholas Wleughels in the costume of Gilles*; red chalk. Städelsches Kunstinstitut, Frankfurt am Main

10. Watteau: Studies of five children, two heads, and a cloaked figure; red and white chalks. The Louvre, Paris

way that painting moves between twin poles; and it is in this that its continued vitality may be found.

Look again at *The Music Party*. The landscape looks back to the god-haunted glades of the golden age and forward to the very best of Fragonard. Impressionism is foreshadowed in the treatment of light, in the way in which that element unifies the image. The colonnade owes much to Rubens's *Coronation of Maria de' Medici*, which the young Watteau had often seen in the Luxembourg Palace. The colour owes much to Veronese. The figures, perfect or botched, are a little imperfectly disposed in space – especially the disproportionate dog – compared with such wonderful achievements as *The*

Ball in the Colonnade in the Dulwich Gallery or – greatest of all – *L'Enseigne de Gersaint* in Berlin.

Why, then, did I choose this picture which I have been so ready to criticize in detail ? I did not do it capriciously, or perhaps I did. If I did, it was a Watteauesque caprice on my part. It is because, for no reason that I can adequately explain, I am haunted by it. It is in this that Watteau's magic defies analysis. There is a slim thread of this special magic running right through the history of painting, and it is curiously consistent. Giorgione had it and having cast his spell over the art of the Venetians, died young. Watteau in a mere twelve years of maturity threw a net of imagery over the whole eighteenth century, far beyond Paris, and he set his scene in just that Cythera, those Elysian Fields, inhabited by Giorgione's lute-player and his friends in the *Concert Champêtre*, now in the Louvre. The young Gainsborough and the young Goya both visited the place and went their different ways. It is an enchanted place.

When I was asked to choose a picture to discuss I said at once *Les Charmes de la vie* – the original title of *The Music Party*. When I went again to look at it I could not think why I should have chosen it rather than the Dulwich picture or even two others in the same room at the Wallace Collection. It is a mystery to me. Some pictures haunt the mind in a special way. Giorgione, the greatest of all such alchemists, defies explanation at any level, Watteau at one. His magic haunts the mind when one is *not* looking at his pictures.

*

Biographical note

Jean Antoine Watteau was born at Valenciennes, in Flanders, on 10 October 1684. Little is known of his childhood, but he was early apprenticed to a local artist named Jacques Albert Gérin. In 1702 Watteau went to Paris, where for two years he lived in dire poverty, making his living as a copyist of Dutch cabinet pictures. At the age of twenty he joined the studio of Claude Gillot, a highly talented and versatile artist whose passion for the theatre, and pleasure in the *commedia dell'arte*, showed the young Watteau where his own visual material would lie. The turning-point in Watteau's career occurred in 1709 when he left Gillot after a quarrel and was engaged by Claude Audrun. Audrun was Concierge of the Luxembourg Palace and was able to give Watteau access to the great Rubens cycle of paintings there. The art of Rubens was the greatest single pictorial influence on Watteau through his life, and the full flower of Rubens's genius must first have been revealed to him in the Luxembourg Palace. From the gardens of this palace, he also drew the landscape in which he would often set the gallant company of his figures, and from Audrun, too, he learned a taste for the exotic and a mastery of rococo caprices. In this year also, at the age of twenty-five, he entered for the Prix de Rome and secured second prize. He did not, however, visit Italy, but returned in the same year to Valenciennes, obtaining the money for this journey from the sale of a small picture to the dealer Sirois. The details of this period of Watteau's life are obscure, and in 1710 he was back in Paris, living with Sirois, who gave him free board and lodging, and his career was fully launched. But in 1711, when he was twenty-seven, the first mention is made of the tuberculosis which was to kill him, exactly ten years later. The effect of this disease, then called *la maladie de la langueur*, seems to have increased Watteau's restlessness and the sombre and melancholy temperament ascribed to him by his friend Caylus, for he became increasingly careless of the techniques of painting; but it may also have sharpened the piercing sensitivity which contributed so much to his greatness. In 1712 he was made an *Agrégé de l'Académie* and should at this time have submitted his *morceau de réception* or diploma picture. This he did not do and despite frequent reminders of this obligation, he delayed his submission until 1717, when on 28 August he took his oath in the presence of the Regent. As an especial honour, Watteau had been allowed to select his own subject for the diploma work and he submitted the first version of *L'Embarquement pour l'Île de Cythère*. Despite the lengthy delay in making his submission he painted the picture in a few days. Unsure of how to describe this novel picture, the Academy received it as a *fête galante* and without great interest. The expression '*fête galante*', which has become synonomous with the painting of Watteau, was first used to describe his work on that occasion; and this remained his constant theme and that of many of his imitators. The years between 1715 and 1719 were the period of Watteau's greatest output and in the latter year, with his disease fatally advanced, he made a visit to London. It is possible he did so in order to consult Dr Mead, a doctor who, apart from his fashionable practice, was a notable collector. Watteau may or may not have painted two pictures for Dr Mead while he was in London and it seems he made a number of drawings, but his health became markedly worse, and he returned to Paris. During the autumn of 1720 he worked with feverish speed and intensity. During the final weeks of his life he was tormented by remorse for sins he felt himself to have committed. He asked for the return of pictures and drawings which he considered erotic and destroyed them. To the last, he continued to paint, completing a *Christ on the Cross* (now lost) a few days before his death. On 18 July 1721 he died, at the age of thirty-six, in the arms of his friend the picture dealer Gersaint.

The historical period

The period through which Watteau lived coincides with the long reign of the Sun King, Louis XIV. In one sense, Watteau is the epitome of the *fin de siècle* artist and the romantic mood of his pictures is properly elegiac. At the same time, he represents the first vigorous stirring of a new spirit which, under the banner of Rubens, would reach its final climax in Delacroix. He came to fame under the patronage of a new élite which, impatient of the frigid gloom dominating the court of Versailles under the puritanical influence of Mme de Maintenon, had centred on Paris. Although he lived for only six years after the death of Louis XIV in 1715, he represents the *avant-garde* of the Regency period and the influence which formed it, rather than the austere grandeurs of the court at Versailles. The reign of Louis XIV had lasted sixty-seven years.

11. Watteau: *The Music Lesson,* oil painting on panel 6⅞ by 8⅞ inches (17·5 by 22·5 cms.)(the figure of Mezzetin in this painting and *The Music Party* clearly derive from the same drawing). The Wallace Collection, London

Within another such span of years, the French monarchy and its aristocracy would stand on the brink of complete and final dissolution. But during those intervening years, until the revolution swept the fashions of the eighteenth century into temporary oblivion, the art of painting in France was dominated by the spirit of Antoine Watteau. His immediate followers, J. B. Pater (1696–1736) and N. Lancret (1690–1743), owed everything to him, and later in the century Boucher and Fragonard based their art upon the elegant tradition established by Watteau, as did a host of minor artists. In

England, Gainsborough and Turner both stood in his debt and in Spain the early pastorals of Goya stem indirectly from Watteau. The Revolution, and the neo-classic art it sponsored, condemned the frivolity of Watteau and his followers. Yet it was Ingres, the neo-classic master, who began the restoration of Watteau to favour even while disapproving of him, and Ingres' arch-rival Delacroix who completed Watteau's restoration. Both artists copied Watteau drawings.

History of *The Music Party*

The picture was engraved by P. Aveline in 1730 (it then belonged to a M. Glucq) under the title *Les Charmes de la vie*, a title which seems preferable to its present one. Its date is uncertain, but the man on the left, in a red cap, has been identified as a portrait of Nicholas Wleughels, a Flemish painter with whom Watteau shared a house between 1718 and 1719. The landscape is partly factual and partly fantastic. The great pillars recall Rubens's *Coronation of Maria de' Medici*, whereas the vista seems to represent the Champs-Élysées with the Chaussée d'Antin in the background.

Practically every detail used by Watteau in the composition of the figures has been paired to an existing drawing, with the exception of the standing musician at the centre, who occurs in much the same pose in *The Music Lesson* [11].

The painting was bought by the fourth Marquis of Hertford between 1847 and 1856, and passed thence to the Wallace Collection, bequeathed to the nation in 1897.

Books for reference

Barker, G., *Antoine Watteau*, 1939

Goncourt, E. and J., *French Eighteenth Century Painters*, trans. and ed. by R. Ironside, 1948

Huyghe, R., and Adhémar, H., *Watteau*, Paris, 1950

Parker, K. T., and Mathey, J., *Antoine Watteau; Catalogue complet de son œuvre dessiné*, two vols., Paris, 1958

Parker, K. T., *The Drawings of Antoine Watteau*, 1931

Catalogue: Paintings and Drawings, Wallace Collection, London, 1928

The Martyrdom of St Sebastian

Pollaiuolo

The National Gallery owns almost two thousand paintings, and *The Martyrdom of St Sebastian*, an Italian picture of the fifteenth century, is not one of the most famous possessions of this incomparably rich collection. It lacks the magic poetry of a Titian or a Rembrandt, the meticulous clarity of a Jan van Eyck, the calm composure of a Poussin, or the homely atmosphere of a Constable. In fact, it has been called by one critic 'a not very attractive picture'. Not everybody will share this view. The picture has qualities of its own, even if they are not obvious at first sight. I find this picture, whenever I see it, immensely exciting and absorbing, for I read it as a moving document of artistic endeavour. After all, there are many reasons why we go to galleries and are captivated by pictures, and there are no wrong reasons for liking them.

The Martyrdom of St Sebastian was painted in 1475 and reveals many of the interests which occupied Florentine artists during a century which changed the face of European painting. Antonio Pollaiuolo – and he must have been the designer of this picture; his younger brother Piero seems only to have helped with the execution of certain parts – was wide awake to current problems, and this large altar-piece is his serious and sincere attempt to give his answer to them.

At first sight, the picture does not seem very subtle. St Sebastian, in the centre, is tied to a stake; six archers in various attitudes are grouped round him; and these human figures form a kind of pyramid with the saint's head at the apex. An interesting device has been used to avoid repetition and monotony: on either side of the saint the archers correspond to each other, but in reverse, so to speak: the one on the extreme left is seen from the front, his opposite number on the right is seen from the back, and so on. The two outer archers stand with their feet apart, but the two in the foreground, nearest to the stake – the ones bending down and winding their crossbows – have their feet together; they bend their knees outward and hold their bows between their legs. Thus, there is both order and subtlety. The artist has taken care to give a convincing account of a dramatic action, naturally performed; but he has disciplined his observation for the sake of strict pictorial order.

That applies not only to details: it applies to the general effect of the whole picture. If one looks at it from a distance of about ten feet or a little more, the saint and his torturers stand out three-dimensionally against the landscape background. The scene looks as real as if we saw it before our very eyes. But while looking at it, we become aware of a rather over-tidy arrangement, of something unnatural in the grouping, of something stilted in the movement. We become aware of the diagonals which hold together the group of human figures – of this light triangle of bodies which is set against a darker background composed of a number of horizontal strips. Antonio Pollaiuolo must have tried to make every limb, face, gesture, every detail of the landscape, as natural as possible. Yet the whole scene is far more rigid, far more balanced, than any such horrible event could possibly have been. Surely, here is a contradiction, the clash between the realistic detail and the obvious desire to contain such realism within a painting in which close attention to the qualities of design determines the final place of even the smallest detail.

I must try to explain how this conflict arose for Antonio Pollaiuolo, and why I call *The Martyrdom of St Sebastian* a document of artistic endeavour. Artists in the early fifteenth century were searching for means of translating what the eye had seen into lifelike pictures. They observed the world around them, they studied the human body, and they wondered how they could achieve an illusion of reality. During the fourteen-twenties a Florentine architect, Filippo Brunelleschi, made the most important discovery in this respect: perspective. He established certain geometrical laws and found practical methods which allowed artists to solve this problem. As his biographer put it:

He enabled artists to represent correctly and rationally the differences in size seen by the human eye in near and far objects as buildings, plains, mountains, and landscapes of all kinds, and to give figures and everything else a suitable size corresponding to the distance at which they are seen.

Perspective, as Brunelleschi and his followers taught it, had to do with the rendering of objects in space. Pictures should conform to visual perception. If we look once more at Pollaiuolo's painting we shall see how convincingly he indicates recession by diminishing the scale of his figures. There are large executioners in the foreground, smaller ones behind the stake, and still smaller soldiers with their horses in the background. In the often-quoted words of Alberti, such pictures have been compared to a view through an open window.

The attention paid to perspective is only one sign that Florentine artists were passionately interested in nature. They also studied the human body, its anatomy, its mechanics, and its proportions. Previously, painters had been satisfied with traditional formulas handed down from generation to generation and faithfully studied from pattern books. Now artists began to draw from the model and to pose the model. Leone Battista Alberti, another Florentine, has recorded what, in his opinion, a painting should achieve. He was not only a scholar and amateur artist himself, he was – most important of all – a close friend of the most progressive artists of his day and knew what was being discussed in their studios. His treatise on painting, written in 1435, is dedicated to Brunelleschi. *The Martyrdom of St Sebastian* was painted forty years later. But Alberti's rules still held good, and his precise formulations throw more light on Antonio Pollaiuolo's methods than many a modern analysis of this picture.

'One divides painting into three parts,' Alberti writes, 'and we have taken this division from Nature: contour, composition, and light.' Having given these terms of reference, he explains each of them in turn. Contour must be a clear and simple delineation of the boundaries of each figure. Antonio followed this precept almost too closely: each of his seven figures is clearly circumscribed; they do not overlap: they barely touch each other.

Next comes composition. But by this term Alberti does not mean

12. Detail from *The Martyrdom of St Sebastian*. The soldier winding his crossbow is best described in the words of Vasari: 'one sees the swelling of the veins and muscles and the holding of the breath to gather force'

exactly what we mean when we use the word today. Composition is a method by which the individual elements are fitted together in a picture. That requires, above all, close attention to the anatomy and correct proportion of the human figure, and Alberti advises artists to begin by drawing the skeleton, to add the muscles, and, finally, to clothe this framework with flesh and skin. There was hardly an artist in Florence who took this advice more literally than Antonio Pollaiuolo; and every one of his figures bears witness to his sure knowledge of anatomy. If we look a little more closely, for example, at the shoulder and arms of the archer winding his crossbow [12], we shall understand why Vasari, the sixteenth-century historian of art, wrote that Pollaiuolo, who dissected many corpses, was the first to represent the correct action of the muscles. We can see the swelling of the veins and muscles, Vasari says, of the archer winding his bow, and even the manner in which he is holding his breath.

But composition, as far as Alberti was concerned, was much more than simply a matter of giving the correct physical appearance of the human figure. This figure must also be in character: athletes must be athletic in every limb. Hence, in Pollaiuolo's picture, the fine contrast between the sturdy executioners with their taut muscles, and the slimmer, slightly feminine figure of the saint: the difference is intentional, and for Alberti – or any follower of his – it would have been ludicrous to design a hefty saint with a meek and submissive face. This meek expression, which may strike us as inappropriate, was chosen deliberately, because it was one of the conventions of this period for suggesting saintliness. In Alberti's own words: 'All figures, both in size and function, must be related to the story they represent.'

For it is a picture telling a story convincingly which Alberti has in mind; and so composition means for him still more than simply formal order: composition for him is akin to appropriateness. Consequently, Alberti appreciates variety only as long as every detail appears in its proper place and belongs to the story. The soldiers in the background of the *Martyrdom* are not just there to fill an empty spot in the picture. They, and the triumphal arch on the left, indicate both the time and the place of this incident; they also remind us that the saint had been a commander in the Praetorian Guard.

Pollaiuolo's picture is clear and simple because he used only seven principal figures. There are no extras to obscure the story. 'Just as princes lend weight to their orders by being brief,' Alberti had written, 'a limited number of figures adds not a little dignity to a picture.' And he added that these few figures should be shown in various positions, some standing upright, others sitting, some dressed, others nude. This particular piece of advice Antonio has followed again and turned to the greatest advantage: the action unfolds itself through the various positions and gestures of the six executioners.

Antonio may have been particularly receptive in this respect; he was fascinated by the human figure – that is the human figure in violent action, and the way in which it can be correctly yet pictorially rendered. His only signed engraving shows ten nude men fighting [13]. They take up all sorts of attitudes, some are on the ground and some are stabbing each other. But every individual figure is placed in such a way that the movement of all limbs is easily understood. There are the same kinds of inversions as seen in the archers of the *Martyrdom*. Art historians have done a good deal of ingenious and unsuccessful guesswork about the subject-matter of *The Battle of the Ten Nude Men*. Maybe Antonio was illustrating some legend or other, but I think that can only have been a pretext. From the artist's point of view this print is another demonstration of Alberti's rules, something like a sheet in a pattern book.

In Pollaiuolo's *St Sebastian* the archers are examples of what was later to be called an 'Academy figure', that is a model posed in some interesting attitude for the purpose of study and instruction. True, they fulfil a function in the telling of the story, but they do so a little too obviously; they are also variations on the theme: the human figure in motion. We are hardly surprised to learn that, within his lifetime, drawings by Antonio were handed round artists' studios and copied by students.

Of course, not every artist in Florence shared Antonio's pre-occupation; Botticelli also painted a St Sebastian [14] and his picture

13. *The Battle of the Ten Nude Men*; engraving by Antonio Pollaiuolo. The British Museum

probably antedates Pollaiuolo's by only a year. How much stronger is the Gothic tradition in Botticelli's figure. The anatomy is roughly correct, but the sway of the figure, the elongated limbs, the linear design, all this takes precedence over the acute observation of muscles and joints.

Alberti spoke of contour, composition, and light as the basic requirements of painting; but when he mentions light, we must not think of it in modern terms. He means simply that he wants painters to study modelling by light and shade: in this too Antonio Pollaiuolo followed him. The saint and the archers stand out light against a dark background; each figure is strongly modelled, and in this way

Pollaiuolo conveys to us a real feeling for the third dimension. It is worth while studying this particular device a little more closely. The archers in the foreground are more strongly modelled than the men shooting at the saint from behind. The soldiers in the foreground stand on one common footline and move in one plane, and the same is true of the two in the background. Each of these planes in turn is set parallel to the darker background, for the footlines of the executioners run parallel to the lower edge of the picture. Hence Pollaiuolo's painting has a good deal in common with a Greek or Roman relief in which figures stand before the ground much in the same way. That is precisely the impression the artist must have wanted to convey. For Alberti had urged painters to pay attention to this effect: 'Connoisseurs and laymen will praise a face which stands out like something cut with a chisel', he had written.

Yet *The Martyrdom of St Sebastian* is not a stone relief; in fact there is a good deal of colour in it, but it is applied in a particular way, and again Alberti may be held responsible for this. For the variety of colours, the striped loincloth, the cloaks, accord well with his demand to increase the beauty of one colour by setting it by the side of another. Pink, green, and sky-blue were colours he recommended – and Antonio used these a good deal.

In his treatise on painting, Alberti had not spoken of landscape and its treatment, but we know that he experimented with a kind of box, something like a camera obscura, in order to demonstrate 'high mountains, distant views, the infinite expanse of the sea stretching to the horizon and disappearing in a haze'. Again, this may help us to understand Pollaiuolo's beautiful and truly remarkable landscape background. The *Martyrdom* is not set within this piece of Tuscan scenery; it happens in front of it, as before a back-drop on a stage. There is no real relationship between foreground and scenery. The stake is set up on a high hillock, there is a sharp fall away to the valley behind, but there is no middle ground to act as a link. The landscape is just such a distant view as mentioned in the account of Alberti's demonstration: it is a kind of pictorial map seen from high above, there is a river winding towards the horizon, there is a large

14. Botticelli: *St Sebastian*, probably painted a year earlier than the Pollaiuolo picture. Formerly Staatliche Museen, Berlin

expanse of valley, and there are far-away blue mountains. All this seems to be almost a picture by itself [15].

I think we can see how this came about. Antonio Pollaiuolo wanted to embody in his picture everything Alberti, the most advanced art critic, had recommended. But he did not succeed in fusing all the divergent elements into an absolutely satisfactory picture. Really too many new things had been discovered. But let us not be unnecessarily hard on this daring painter. After all, he was one of the first Italians to attempt such an ambitious background, and some of the details are lovely – for example, the river and the weir on the right.

I began by calling Pollaiuolo's picture a document of artistic endeavour. The master had grown up at a time when the conquest of reality was the all-pervading passion of painters. The works of Masaccio and Donatello were there to be followed, and Alberti had codified this tradition in his book. Now, in 1475, all this is at Antonio's disposal – observation, a respect for pictorial values, dignity, and restraint. But he never forgets that he is making a religious picture. The dignity and saintly suffering of Sebastian have their counterpart in the dignity and serenity of the composition, which presages the much more subtle art of Raphael and his generation.

*

Biographical note

The Pollaiuolo brothers were Florentines; Antonio was born about 1431 or 1432 and Piero seems to have been his junior by ten years. Antonio was trained as a goldsmith, possibly by Ghiberti's son Vittorio. He was much influenced by Donatello, particularly after the sculptor's return from Padua in 1453. By 1457 Antonio was well established and was given his first important commission: a silver reliquary for the Baptistery (Museum of the Opera del Duomo, Florence). Together with a relief representing the birth of the Baptist, on the silver altar in the same place (in the same museum), this is all that survives of Antonio's work as a goldsmith. But he also worked in

15. Detail of landscape background from *The Martyrdom of St Sebastian*, rendered with truth and delicacy reminiscent of Leonardo

bronze. The small group of *Hercules and Antaeus* (now in the Bargello, Florence) [16] once belonged to the Medici; and a number of other statuettes have been attributed to him. There are also two bronze monuments for tombs: in 1484 Antonio was called to Rome to make the tomb for Sixtus IV (SS. Grotte Vaticane, Rome) and in 1492 he was commissioned to make another for Innocent VIII (St Peter's, Rome).

According to Vasari much of Antonio's work in precious metals was melted down during times of need and the artist himself decided to turn to painting, in order to achieve more lasting fame. Whatever Antonio's motives, again according to Vasari, he turned to his brother Piero to learn how to handle paints. Modern critics have scorned this statement, but there is nothing extraordinary about it. As a goldsmith Antonio must have been familiar with techniques of drawing; both Vasari and Cellini called him a great draughtsman. All he required from his younger brother was an introduction to the technique of painting.

Piero had been trained as a painter. He is the author of six (of the seven) *Virtues* commissioned in 1469 and 1470 for the Council Chamber of the Mercatanzia (Uffizi, Florence). An altar-piece with the *Coronation of the Virgin* (Church of S. Agostino, San Gimignano) is signed and dated 1483. On the evidence of these works Piero was a minor and hardly competent master. If we look at joint works, such as *The Martyrdom of St Sebastian* or the altar-piece from S. Miniato (Uffizi, Florence), it becomes clear that Piero did his best work when following the designs of his more talented brother.

Piero and Antonio went to Rome in 1484 and Piero assisted his brother with the papal tombs. Antonio died in Rome in 1498, probably shortly after Piero.

Provenance and authorship

The Martyrdom of St Sebastian was acquired by the National Gallery in 1857. Originally it had been in the church of SS. Annunziata in Florence, and Vasari tells us that it had been commissioned in 1475.

The picture is not signed, but early Italian sources call it the work of Piero del Pollaiuolo. Modern authorities have given it to Antonio or have assumed that it is the joint work of the two brothers.

It is said that Vasari named Antonio as the author, but inspection of his text will show that he believed in a collaboration between Antonio and Piero. Vasari lists paintings executed by Piero alone, and those done jointly by Piero and Antonio. He puts the St Sebastian at the end of the latter group, but says in the next sentence:

16. *Hercules and Antaeus,* bronze statuette by Antonio Pollaiuolo. Known to have been in the Medici Palace in 1495, now in the Bargello, Florence

'And this was the most highly praised work ever done by Antonio. This can only mean that the Martyrdom was painted by Piero and Antonio but that the latter's share ranked as his finest achievement in painting. Vasari goes on to tell us that the patron paid Antonio 300 *scudi* for his work. We may therefore conclude that Antonio designed the picture and painted part of it but that he was assisted by his brother. However, it is difficult to decide how the work was shared. We can only agree with the most prudent critic (Martin Davies) in this matter: 'All that can reasonably be said is that the bodies of the two archers in the near middle distance are inferior in execution to the faces and to the five principal figures.'

The St Sebastian legend

St Sebastian was a young nobleman from Narbonne in Gaul, who under Diocletian (A.D. 284–305) commanded a company of the Praetorian Guard. When converted to Christianity he became a fearless defender of his faith. However, the Emperor identified Christianity with disloyalty and ordered Sebastian to be shot with arrows. His executioners left him for dead, but Irene, a Christian Roman lady, discovered that he was only wounded and nursed him back to health. Later Sebastian boldly attacked Diocletian for his cruelty to the Christians and the enraged Emperor had him executed.

Since arrows were regarded as a symbol of the plague, the Saint, having withstood them, became a protector from this dreadful disease.

Books for reference

The best book in English is still Maud Crutwell, *Antonio Pollaiuolo*. More up-to-date is A. Sabatini, *Antonio e Piero del Pollaiuolo*, 1944 (in Italian). There is a concise and instructive biography of Antonio in J. Pope-Hennessy, *Italian Renaissance Sculpture*, 1958, p.316.

Davies, M., *The Early Italian Schools* (National Gallery Catalogue), second ed., 1961, p.443 (for modern attributions, and further references)

Ettlinger, L. D., 'Pollaiuolo's Tomb of Sixtus IV', *Journal of the Warburg and Courtauld Institutes*, vol. XVI, 1953, p.238 ff.

Murray, P., *An Index of Attributions made in Tuscan Sources before Vasari*, 1959, p.133 (for early attributions to Piero)

Vasari, G., *Le Vite de' più eccelenti pittori* etc., ed. G. Milanesi, vol. III, 1878, p.292 f.

View from Louveciennes

Camille Pissarro

This is a picture of a real road; it was painted from one particular point on the side of the road and was almost certainly carried through in a few days. We can be fairly certain, too, that while he was painting it Pissarro believed that he was being governed by the evidence of his eyes; that the painting was, in other words, based closely upon his impressions of the place at the time.

I should think it would be impossible to look at this picture without feeling a sense of freedom: and also a sense of Pissarro's attitude to the visible world, his affirmation of it and his insistence on it as a source of luxury and delight.

It is a spring morning, the sunlight cool, crisp, putting a veiled glitter over the road, the bare branches of the trees, the blossom that speckles them. In places the light falls in depth over the tops of the trees in a sort of luminous fur. An endless variety of textures, rhythms, and scales are brought to equal terms on the surface of the canvas: bare branches, distant masonry, clouds, blossom, leaves, earth, blue sky, the column-like figure of the peasant woman – and all are painted with the same flat, unmodelled flakes of paint.

It is this feature, this all-over unity, more than felicities of subject-matter or decorative effects of colour, which gives Impressionist painting its air of freedom. (I mean by Impressionism the style practised by Monet [17], Renoir, and Pissarro between the late eighteen-sixties and the early eighties.) The Impressionists saw the world in terms of light; and they saw light in terms of opaque paint. Impressionism proposed a new view of drawing, for its definitions were achieved without the flourish, the rhythmical systems, of earlier art. It does not wrestle with the forms as all modelled art does; there is no show of muscle. Nor does anything escape because it is left at a distance: everything is accessible, touched

---

*This painting is part of the Lane Bequest and among the group due to be lent to the Municipal Gallery, Dublin, for five years from late 1965.

17. Monet: *The Train in the Snow*, 1875. Musée Marmottan, Paris

by the eye and kept, because it is miraculously harmonized. No other style has quite the same power to project us into the outside world. To look at this painting of Pissarro's is to refresh over and over again our experience of outdoor space. Space is expressed in every aspect of the picture, and each stroke of paint is chosen for its resonance against its neighbour – and also for its active contribution to the whole. The double part played by each fragment of paint is essential to the life of the picture, its space and light.

To understand the special qualities of Impressionist painting, consider another landscape with the same theme – Hobbema's *The Avenue* [18]. In the seventeenth-century picture the main relationship between the land and the sky is expressed in a simple contrast: dark land, light sky. All the smaller forms are worked out inside the limits of this main contrast. But in the Pissarro the relationship

18. Hobbema: *The Avenue*, 1689. The National Gallery, London

is far more complex: it is based less on a contrast than on a subtle interlocking. Pissarro's sky is no back-drop, nor is the road a stage – the two interlock in an inclusive relationship, so that, although we are never in doubt as to how far away anything is, at the same time we seem to be drawn into the picture as we are drawn into the real world with our eyes. This is not simply because of perspective; it is due more to the painter's all-round continuous awareness of space, expressed in an endless series of affinities, a series of webs in which each coloured link contributes its necessary value.

The blue uniform of the postman on the left seems to concentrate the patch of blue sky over his head; while the white blossom and the creamy walls of the barn to the right of him do the same with the white clouds above them. A chain of such relationships stretches from the postman on the left of the picture to the blossom on the right,

19. Corot: *The Sèvres Road*, 1855. The Louvre, Paris

and it forms a sort of flattened pyramid with its apex in the eaves of a white building on the sky-line; and this slow, expansive shape seems to project itself upwards into the sky as though great arms were mapping out the position of clouds overhead.

This is only one aspect of the relationship between land and sky, as it is worked out in fairly large forms; the same process continues even down to individual strokes. A small section of the foreground of Hobbema's picture is a self-contained incident, rich in itself. In the Pissarro each fragment of paint, although it appears to mean less in itself, to be more abstract, is invested with the same luminosity as the sky. You seem to get less – and more – from each stroke: less description but a richer equivalence of space and light; less incident but a weightier content.

By 1870, the year this picture was painted, Pissarro had arrived at the position he was to occupy for the next ten years. He had modelled himself upon Corot when he had first started to paint in the country-side around Paris, and it was from Corot [19] that Pissarro learned to see his subjects in terms of a tonal ensemble. He learned to work directly from his impressions and to allow the immediate experience in front of the scene to be the guiding factor by which all the other aspects of the picture were regulated. And it was from Corot, too, that Pissarro had his first intimations of the tradition of classical composition which he was later to bring to life in such an extra-ordinary way.

But there was another ingredient in Pissarro's formation as a painter, more active and more difficult to assimilate than the purely technical example of Corot. I mean realism. Realism is always associated with the name of Courbet – because he used the word as a personal battle-cry. But it was far too wide a tendency to be de-fined by one man. Briefly, it was concerned with treating subjects from contemporary life rather than from history and literature: and it wanted to treat them without idealizing them, describing them just as they were, without relating them to a traditional canon of form.

Neither Courbet, nor Millet, nor Daumier painted in the open air. It was not until the eighteen-sixties that their younger followers carried realism to its logical conclusion in this way. It is difficult for us now to appreciate the novelty of open-air painting in the history of painting as a whole, or to realize how controversial it was when it first was done. It was a programme of revolt: the *plein air* painters, and I think Pissarro in particular, saw themselves moving away from the deceiving shadows of the studio into the light of day. They turned away from the snobbish play-acting implied in the official paintings of history and mythology. Instead they looked into the real world, where everything, even the most mundane thing, can be seen as having some human significance.

Open-air painting was a democratic tendency (and was recognized as such by its opponents) because the subjects it treated were available to everybody's eyes and anyone could relate the pictures to their own experience. And also it was individual to an unprecedented degree: each work represented an individual choice of view and a degree of personal improvisation. Indeed, the picture as a whole only takes on value in relation to its personal content: where a lay onlooker might ask in front of an earlier picture 'What is it about?', he might ask in front of a *plein airist* picture 'What has the artist seen in this subject?'

Of course one cannot talk about the realist tendencies of the eighteen-fifties and sixties as though they amounted to a single-minded, clearcut whole. Many ideas that evolved together out of revolt against the academic tradition turned out to be difficult to reconcile as time went on. Painting from nature, for example, proved to be almost irreconcilable with the exploration of realist ideas, because, to put it roughly, the more closely a painter pursued the appearance of things, the more involved he was bound to become in his own subjective impressions of them; and the more subjective his painting became, the less room there was in it for general communication about the nature of his subject-matter. In fact it was the increased subjectivity of Impressionism which really distinguished it from realism.

One of the general intentions of realism was to record contemporary man in his environment, to paint not so much the individual as the circumstances that made him. Pissarro and Degas were the only members of the Impressionist group to follow up this intention. To Monet, for example, the busiest street was interesting mainly as an optical effect in which the human element was merely one ingredient among many: we could almost imagine that he hardly reflected whether he was painting grass or pavement, parasol or trouser leg. The outward aspects of the subject have become absorbed in the seeing of them. Pissarro's peasants are painted with as clear a sense of who they are and what they are doing as Degas' washerwomen or dancers. But where Degas will concentrate upon a gesture or a posture which is expressive of habit, or training, or necessity, with Pissarro

20. Pissarro: *La Route de Louveciennes*, 1870. The Louvre, Paris

we are made aware of the whole landscape and its bearing on the people who move in it and are governed by it.

Whenever our eyes roam over the surface of the *View from Louveciennes*, exploring foliage, sky, the warm expanses of the road or the violety-grey spaces, they always return, as though to a key, to the figures. Above all, we return to the column-like back of the peasant woman. There is a certain heightening of tension round Pissarro's figures, an alertness, as though where men stood the air was just

21. Poussin: *The Gathering of the Ashes of Phocion*, 1648. The Earl of Derby, Knowsley, Lancs

that much clearer, the ground that much more firm. Consider the quickening in the drawing round the woman's figure here, the tense, box-like interval between her and the wall on her right, occupied so exactly by the roadman. The sense of scale between the woman, the little tree, and the man, so grand and so utterly real, is one of the most perfect things in the painting of the nineteenth century.

It was necessary at the time, and it has become conventional since, to talk about *plein airism* as though it was nothing else but a campaign against the time-worn clichés of the academic tradition. But it can also be seen as a campaign to reconstitute some of the traditions of painting in a new context, and to bring them back to life in front of nature. Some of the subjects painted by the Impressionists indicate the first view, and others the second. Snow, for instance, or sunlight on broken water, were clearly conditions of nature that were painted in order to claim certain unprecedented effects for the language of painting. On the other hand, a road or a street seen in perspective, a theme painted time after time by Monet, Renoir, and Sisley, as well as by Pissarro, was clearly turned to so often simply because it offered in real life some of the formal elements of classical landscape composition.

Pissarro in particular was concerned with bringing the modern anti-traditional aspect of his work into some sort of relation with the tradition of landscape painting. And for him the road-in-perspective theme was an endlessly fruitful obsession. In his many series of views looking along roads he explored every nuance, every possible permutation, of construction. Perspective was the agency by which the most mundane scene could be given a classical articulation, could be seen in terms of proportion and interval. Thus in so simple a picture as *La Route de Louveciennes* [20] in the Louvre, the fabric of the composition is carried by the horizontal which runs from the horizon at the far end of the road through the wall on the left, and the verticals of the trees and buildings. The sloping angles of the roofs and the shadows on the road drive one's eyes into the strongest vertical of all, the two figures advancing down the road, the key point in the picture.

Although this ordinary scene is a world away from the idealized construction of, for instance, Poussin's *The Gathering of the Ashes of Phocion* [21], yet it partakes of something of its nobility: its spaces, so different in their meaning, are carved out with a kindred austerity, a similar clarity. But among the thousand contrasts between the two pictures there is one which is essential: the standing figure in the centre of the Poussin leads us into the picture with his gesture; we notice particularly how his figure seems to indicate the closed and authoritative form of the temple that stands immediately above him. We are an audience in front of a proscenium arch. In the Pissarro the vertical accent formed by the figures corresponds with the straight edge of the pavement in front of them at their feet: this is vertical

22. Pissarro: *La Côte du Jallais à Pontoise,* 1867. Metropolitan Museum, New York

precisely because the painter is standing on it: the strongest accent in the picture, the one that determines every other feature, aligns us with the painter's own position in front of his motif.

Thus for Pissarro perspective moves outwards and inwards at the same time: it is the agency which orders the world in the onlooker's eye, which defines and at the same time overcomes distance, the very hallmark of human vision. There is nothing theoretical or doctrinaire in the way he uses it; merely an absorbed attention to the way things get bigger and smaller or line up in the eye as you move about. In the Pontoise landscapes of the late eighteen-sixties

23. Pissarro: *Une Matinée de juin, hauteurs de Pontoise*, 1873.

these alignments and correspondences in perspective provide the dominant theme [22, 23], and later, when Pissarro's art reached its climax in the eighteen-seventies, this sense of the dual power of perspective, pointing inwards as well as outwards, is no less strong. But now colour and light and perspective are seen as having an integral meaning. Distance is seen not as a nostalgic haze but precisely: nearness and farness, 'here' and 'right out there' are brought together exactly in the same structure.

In the *View from Louveciennes* the painter is standing on the grassy verge at the left; he sights down it; the bush facing him seems to measure up to him. To the right he takes a great level sweep which includes the orchard below the road and much of the wooded hillside beyond it. These two movements, up and down the grass verge, left and right across the road, complement each other and provide the picture with its scale. They interlock continually: the shadows across the road on the left reach out towards the hedge opposite, defining the width of the road, locking it into the column of green and brown that the grass verge makes. Right across the picture the trunks of trees divide up the spaces of the orchard into compartments, each interval perfectly felt, each like a self-contained country, holding a promise. The clearest of these compartments is that between the woman and the tree trunk facing the painter. This is made into a square by the shadow on the road and the aqueduct on the sky line.

The woman's figure gives scale to the whole picture. We feel that the light that saturates the wide road and glitters in the orchard is concentrated on her, as though the russet of her jacket or the whiteness of her cap were the sum total of it. She dominates the square compartment ahead, where the tree not yet in leaf opens like a fan in front of her. Her size and her warm colour are echoed in the trunk of the tree that faces the painter, and the arches of the aqueduct against the sky are like repetitions of her white cap.

Pissarro was never to lose his sense of commitment to what he painted, nor did his responses to it lose their poignancy. There is a wonderful generosity of vision here, an evenness; although he might ascribe a key role to one part of the picture rather than another, it was never at the expense of any aspect of his subject. Each selection was an enhancement of the whole. Each mark that he made, always so eager yet so unflourished, tense yet sober, was a claim for the real world, an affirmation.

*

Biographical note

Camille Pissarro was born in Saint-Thomas in the then Danish West Indies in 1830, the son of a French-Jewish merchant. He was educated at Passy near Paris at a school whose headmaster was an amateur painter, an admirer of Corot. Back in Saint-Thomas in 1847, Pissarro entered his father's business for a while, then, falling in with a Danish painter called Fritz Melbye, he left home for Caracas, where he devoted all his time to painting.

On the advice of his father, Pissarro returned to Paris with the object of studying under an academic master. He arrived there in

1855. It was a significant moment. The Exposition Universelle was open and he was able to see the richest cross-section of modern European art ever gathered together. Of French painters it included not only the academic stars of the day but also Ingres, Delacroix, and the painters of Barbizon. At the same time Courbet was showing fifty canvases in his own one-man 'Pavillon du Réalisme'.

It is characteristic of Pissarro that he made no effort to place himself on the rungs of the official ladder and instead approached Corot, who was by no means a popular painter then. Corot encouraged him and gave him advice and for several years they were on terms of friendship. Pissarro worked at the École des Beaux-Arts for a short time only and he was soon established in the country painting landscapes and scenes of peasant life. He first exhibited in the Salon in 1859 and it was in this year that he met Claude Monet, then working at the Académie Suisse. Pissarro contributed to the Salon des Refusés in 1862, and throughout the 1860s he was in touch with Monet, Cézanne, Renoir, and Sisley.

By 1865 his style had been affected by the broad realism of Courbet. It was as an exemplar of the realist movement that Zola noticed his work at the Salon of 1866:

An austere and serious kind of painting, an extreme concern for truth and accuracy, a rugged and strong will. You are a great blunderer, sir – you are an artist I like.

The Franco-Prussian war found Pissarro at Louveciennes, a village near Paris. He left as the Prussians advanced and arrived in London later in the year. Here he found Monet and Daubigny and through the latter was introduced to Paul Durand-Ruel, the dealer who was to be virtually the Impressionists' only support for years to come. On his return to France, Pissarro found that the Prussians had destroyed over a thousand of his canvases. In 1872 he moved to Pontoise (he had already worked there before the war) and it was here, during the next eight years, that he reached his highest point as a painter.

By 1873 it had become clear that the Batignolles painters had nothing to hope for from either the official Salon or, for the time being, from Durand-Ruel. It was in this situation that they organized the first of their independent exhibitions which were to focus public attention on the Impressionist movement. To Monet, Renoir, and the rest, these exhibitions were simply stopgap expedients; to Pissarro they were much more. He alone never showed at the Salon again. He was the only one of the group to contribute to all eight of the Impressionist exhibitions and he was the only one to make serious efforts to hold the group together. It is clear that to him the notion of collective action on the part of painters had an intrinsic value and it was one which related to his beliefs in general. Pissarro was of the extreme left, a friend of Jean Grave and an admirer of Kropotkin for whose pamphlet, *Temps nouveaux*, he designed a cover. His letters make it clear that he valued the modernity of Impressionism and its anti-bourgeois content:

I firmly believe that something of our ideas, born as they are of the anarchist philosophy, passes into our works ....

His rural subjects were expressions of value and reflect something of the agrarian idealism of the anarchist left.

Somewhat older than most of his friends, Pissarro had a unique position among them as a teacher. He helped to give a direction when the central issue was that of *plein air* versus the studio. Pissarro and Monet painted together in 1860 and Monet later acknowledged his debt. During the seventies at Pontoise, Cézanne, Guillaumin, and later Gauguin, all worked at his side. He was extremely sensitive to talent in whatever quarter. 'Originality depends only on the character of the drawing and the vision peculiar to each artist,' he said, and elsewhere, 'I don't care a fig for the method!' Remarks like these which recur in the letters explain his passionate support for Cézanne from the moment when he first met him; for Gauguin, at least until he was engulfed by Symbolism; for Le Douanier Rousseau on his first appearance; for Van Gogh when he arrived in Paris with his *Potato Eaters*. '*Ce fut un père pour moi*', Cézanne said years later and when, at the very end of his life, he was persuaded to show paintings, he identified himself as 'pupil of Pissarro'. Nor did Gauguin conceal his debt:

He looked at everybody, you say! Why not ? Everyone looked at him too, but denied him. He was my master and I do not deny him.

At the beginning of the eighties, Pissarro, in common with most of his colleagues, was in a state of dissatisfaction with his work. He felt that he needed to clarify both his aims and his execution. In 1885 he met Signac and Seurat, and was immediately impressed by their work. Although Seurat was young enough to be his son, Pissarro accepted his criticism of Impressionism. For the next five years he practised a more or less systematic divisionism, believing that with this more controlled approach he was being less romantic and more objective. However, it was a false trail for him and he realized after all that it was curtailing his responses to nature.

In 1884 he settled in a large house in Éragny, further out from Paris, and this was to be his base for the rest of his life. His eldest son Lucien had emigrated to London in 1883 and Pissarro was to visit him there on several occasions. Much of the last decade of his life was circumscribed by a chronic infection in his eye which forced him to work indoors. He painted a number of series of street scenes from hotel windows under these conditions (e.g. *The Boulevard Montmartre at Night*, National Gallery). Pissarro died in Paris in November 1903.

History of the *View from Louveciennes*

Painted about 1870, it is signed C. Pissarro. It was bought from the artist in 1897 by Durand-Ruel, and from him by Sir Hugh Lane in 1905; it passed with the Lane Bequest to the nation in 1917, and remained at the Tate Gallery until 1952, when it was transferred to the National Gallery: under the agreement reached with the Irish authorities in 1959, the picture is one of those in the Lane Bequest which will be lent for alternate periods of five years to the Municipal Gallery, Dublin.

Books for reference

Davies, Martin, *French School* (National Gallery Catalogue),
  second ed., 1957, pp. 167–8

Pissarro, C., *Letters to his Son Lucien*, ed. J. Rewald, 1943

Pissarro, L. R., and Venturi, L., *Camille Pissarro*, 1939

Rewald, J., *The History of Impressionism*, 1946; *Pissarro*, 1963

Virgin and Child with Angels

Duccio

I am going to risk the charge of dwelling on the obvious, and begin by emphasizing the age of this picture. Not that we know it exactly: but let us say about 660 years. It has been for more than a century now in the National Gallery and there, paradoxically, it has lost, probably in the eyes of many beholders, at least much of the very thing which must have done most to preserve it until it came there: its devotional character. This must have kept it safe through long ages when it had no aesthetic interest, together with the fact that, unlike so many less ancient pictures in the Gallery, it may well have always borne the name of the very famous artist who painted it. Nevertheless, it is still something of a miracle that it has survived.

The triptych of which this is the centre panel is more destructible as a whole than any of its parts. Together they make a piece of furniture which is as fragile as can be. If it had been dropped on a marble floor it might have been irretrievably smashed; if it had ever got very damp, it would have fallen to pieces. But the parts have stayed together, and they have come down to us in excellent condition; the only significant damage is due – as is so often the case – to an incompetent attempt at cleaning made more than a century ago. The triptych has remained whole over more than six and a half centuries.

That means that we in England have to think back to the reign of Edward I. It is more appropriate to think of a great adversary of his, Pope Boniface VIII, whose temporal power our Edward did something to diminish. The vast wealth of the Papacy at the outset of the fourteenth century is one of the material facts which brought this picture into existence in Siena. The Sienese got a great part of their riches from banking; and they were bankers above all to the Holy See.

This triptych is a luxury picture if ever there was one. In the first place it was a great luxury to commission it to Duccio, who was certainly the most expensive painter of that day. The Florentine

Cimabue, a more heroic figure, may still have been alive when it was painted; the still more famous Florentine, Giotto, though he was a good deal younger than Duccio, was already by then well known. But those two, who were in more ways than one more adventurous than Duccio and lived probably in a larger, more liberated world, with ideas that needed whole wall-surfaces to contain them, had to go far afield, in all probability at lower prices. Duccio, who is not known to have painted in fresco, could remain in his own house, in a Siena which was at the height of her splendour, picking and choosing the commissions that pleased him best.

The great glory of Siena was her cathedral, which shone forth above the rose-pink brick of the town with its polished black and white marble and was embellished with an array of marble sculptures inside and out. To create the cathedral, architects and sculptors were invited from Pisa and Florence; but in painting the traffic was all the other way. For Florence, Duccio early in his career had painted that tremendous altar-piece, surpassing – so it seems to me – the similar one by Cimabue which confronts it in the Uffizi Gallery in Florence. It comes from Santa Maria Novella, which is incidentally Florence's great Dominican church. Duccio always seems to have done his best for the Dominicans – witness our triptych, in which St Dominic occupies the left wing. For Santa Croce, the Franciscan church in Florence, were painted two great Sienese altar-pieces, of which the remains are now happily in the National Gallery. One is the *Virgin and Child with Six Angels*, which now hangs beside our triptych. That can be catalogued only as the work of a follower of Duccio, though it could well have been ordered from his studio. However, it seems to be the work not so much of a mere assistant as of a considerable artist who followed Duccio closely in his ideas. In fact his hand and character have been detected in other pictures. The other ws oriaginally the high-altar itself of Santa Croce, and this again is connected with Duccio. We know that it used to bear the signature of his closest identifiable follower, Ugolino. Unlike the first picture, this was a great polyptych with many panels, and one can see that those of the predella are virtually simplified copies of Duccio's famous *Maestà*, the high-altar-piece of Siena cathedral. Our triptych by Duccio is probably a little earlier than his *Maestà*.

Yet, however sought after Duccio may have been, it is still possible that the materials of this triptych cost almost as much as the artist received for his work. Gold was a much rarer commodity then, even more expensive than it is now; and several layers of gold covering the whole of the background are a distinguishing feature of this kind of picture. Needless to say, the panels are custom-built, each all in one piece with its frame; and all three, with their frames, were heavily overlaid with gold on the face. The frames are very simple, unlike the florid Gothic frames which were to come into fashion before long and which were sometimes allowed to overwhelm the picture; but originally, probably, they were stamped with patterns and possibly partly painted to enrich and soften their effect. The gold backgrounds to the pictures are delicately engraved with decorative borders, and the haloes are patterned in an even more graceful way.

Against this decorated gold background – and actually after it had been applied – the figures of the principal panel and of its tympanum are painted, mostly in ultramarine blue. Already for centuries the traditional uniform of the Madonna had been a tight-fitting red gown and a loose blue mantle over it. The mantle was nearly always the important garment, and here there is only a glimpse of the gown, at the wrist, where one sees the end of a ruby-coloured sleeve thickly striped with gold. Otherwise and except for her voluminous white linen head-scarf, which the Child has pulled out, the Virgin is enveloped in ultramarine. The scarf and the Child's mauve shift, both more or less diaphanous, are there, like the touch of crimson, mainly as foils to the deep, majestic quality of the blue. Two of the four little angels are in blue, set off by different shades of rose, but the Virgin's blue is purer, both more solid and brighter.

It is the same in the tympanum above, where King David in his dual capacity of prophet and of ancestor to the Redeemer presides over the group of prophets who display the texts in which they foretold the Incarnation. David's crimson robe is largely hidden by a cloak of royal blue sewn with gold stars, while the six prophets are in weaker blues contrasted with other colours. Ultramarine, the warm blue pigment that thus dominates, is made from ground lapis lazuli, a very hard semi-precious rock which had to be brought from even greater distances than gold and was almost as expensive. To get the full extraordinary effect of it, it had of course to be used very pure and with as little medium as possible.

Forgive me for dwelling again upon the obvious. But the blueness of this picture, the clear clarion challenge of the unadulterated ultramarine, and the lesser blues which reinforce it, are a fundamental part of its expression. Their significance is not merely symbolical, like that of the gold stars on the Virgin's mantle, which remind us of various mystical titles such as *stella maris* ('star of the sea') bestowed on her in early times.

I cannot help wondering if blue would have been chosen as the Madonna's colour if her attributes had been fixed in some country bordering on the North Sea instead of on the Mediterranean, or, if it had been, whether the painters would have insisted so much upon it for so long. Certainly to most of the great Italian artists of the Middle Ages and the Renaissance blue was the most inspiring of all the colours, one that they absorbed from nature and breathed out again in their most stimulating and passionate works. Our picture is in Room One at the National Gallery. Walk on through the rooms in their order and see what the Italians made of this colour. In most pictures it is the key colour of the design. In all Duccio's four this has a hieratic significance, and so it has inevitably in the next room filled with pictures painted in the Gothic style by his descendants in the fourteenth century and the early fifteenth. The blue is almost overwhelming in some of their works. Further on, in the pictures of Piero della Francesca, perhaps the greatest Italian Renaissance painter of nature – I mean of the natural complex of form and colour and light – the blue has become atmospheric; but it is still very much there. Everything in his *Baptism* and his *Nativity* seems infused with the blueness of the Mediterranean heavens. Even more so his picture with the single figure of Saint Michael, standing in a blue costume against a blue sky. Walk on, and you find much the same in Leonardo and Raphael and Bronzino, in Titian and Tintoretto, at least in those pictures that have been cleaned.

In Northern art, the blue remained predominant only so long as the purpose of painting was hieratic. Few pictures are bluer than the Madonna panel of the Wilton Diptych, even if it is a thin un-Mediterranean blue. But when naturalism came, northern skies, and perhaps the northern craving for warmth, soon had their effect upon the painter's palette – unless he went to Italy. Few Dutch and English painters made more than a limited use of blue. Rembrandt, the greatest Dutchman, came to eliminate it, almost, from his palette. Reynolds, our one great painter-teacher, made up his mind that the larger masses in all great pictures were in warm colour – even if Gainsborough did make a lusty visual protest against his rival's theory by painting his *Blue Boy*. And so in the late eighteenth century and throughout the nineteenth London restorers gave decent burial to most of the Italian blues by covering them with varnish containing brown or yellow colouring matter.

From these tasteful improvements made by the restorers such panels as those of Duccio were usually exempt. They were saved in the first place by their gold backgrounds. Having no atmosphere as a whole, they could not be brought into line with current taste. These are perhaps the most sophisticated and graceful pictures ever painted, coming at the end of a long, long tradition brought, like the blue probably, from Byzantium; but they were called 'primitive'.

Perhaps Duccio's pictures look a little less 'primitive' to us now that some pictures in the National Gallery by Piero and Leonardo and the early Titian have been cleaned. While I have insisted on the number of years which have passed since this *Madonna* was painted, the gap in time between Duccio and the Renaissance is not a big one. Chronology is always worth thinking about, and it is instructive to realize that Duccio, with his gold backgrounds, and Piero della Francesca, with the perfect atmospheric rendering of space in his *Nativity*, were very little further apart in time than is Turner, with all his romantic imagery culled from nature, from mythology, and several kinds of history, from a painter of 'abstract' pictures today.

There is no better place than the National Gallery to study the break from the tradition of which Duccio is the culmination, for there we have the first painted Madonna of the Renaissance, Masaccio's *Virgin and Child with Angels* from Pisa. By comparing this with Duccio's Madonna one can get good clues to the understanding of each of them. The gold background, with the halo elaborately designed on it, the tremendous blue – these are there still in Masaccio's picture, even if his Madonna is so heavily sculptured that obviously she cannot be contained within such a frame much longer. The discomfort of Masaccio's spirit in the tight jacket of the gilded Gothic panel is almost painful. Had he lived to paint other Madonnas, this would almost certainly have been his last with a gilded background. What is positive and important and new is the perspective of her throne and the deep envelope of atmosphere from which her massive figure is projected towards us. With this picture Renaissance ideas had taken hold of religious painting; which meant that painters were launched upon that course of mixed calculation and observation which was very soon to bring to their art complete power over the third dimension.

I do not want to suggest that Duccio was incapable of representing space or even atmosphere. Only look at his three scenes in the National Gallery from the *Maestà* – 'The Transfiguration' with its bare stage of natural rock, 'The Healing of the Man born Blind' with its urban landscape, 'The Annunciation' with its idyllic palace architecture. The figures in these are on a larger scale than their surroundings, for they are what matters. We are still far from the realistic logic of developed Renaissance design; but Duccio's conception of the value of space and his ability to create it are not very different from that of his younger Florentine contemporary Giotto, who is recognized as the herald of the Renaissance.

Indeed, Duccio is to be recognized as one of the great masters of form. In this Virgin we are studying, what power there is! What majesty! You can enlarge this group to any size you like. If it had been painted in life-size, or if the design had been handed to one of the great mosaic craftsmen from Byzantium to enlarge to three times life-size in the shell over the apse to a cathedral choir, this would have been one of the great monuments of all time. As it is, it is one of the pictures which loses most if it is hung on the walls of a gallery, as one of a row of pictures. One needs to have it alone, above one's head. One should be kneeling before it. Then one could appreciate better the sense of scale which underlies the conception of this quite small figure. It is easier to forget the actual size if one is looking at a reproduction, for then the original might be of any size. One can take one's mind's eye for walks in those folds and loops of the Madonna's drapery, in that great open cave of whiteness made by her head-scarf [24]. What infinity there is in the mere outline of this group against the gold! Not many pictures in the world have more grandeur than this one.

What distinguishes Duccio from Giotto is by no means any lack of grandeur, but his determination to reconcile this illusion of powerful, plastic forms with the fact of a sumptuously decorative surface. Here is the point at which Tuscan painting splits into two schools. Not every Florentine by any means ceased even in the fifteenth century to attempt that reconciliation. Uccello spent his life perhaps in combining the new discoveries of artificial perspective and the logical use of concentrated light with the old love of pattern in brilliant colours and in gold. But no Sienese painter ever accepted the idea that an illusion of space was the paramount ideal. He would have thought it vulgar.

To that extent Duccio and the great Sienese tradition, which he took over while it was still more than half Byzantine and perfected at so early a stage that he may be described as its founder, may seem more in harmony with the ideas of today. After five centuries modern painters have renounced for the most part that power over the third dimension which the painters of the fifteenth and sixteenth centuries were at such pains to acquire; and in the works of many of them the picture surface and its texture are almost everything. Yet, for that very reason, there is really no parallel. For instance, the

24. Detail from the *Virgin and Child with Angels*

tachiste picture of today is, perhaps more than any other kind of picture, a completely integrated surface: I mean that from one edge of the picture to the other, the idea is bound up in the texture ; one cannot think of them apart. Whereas in the Sienese picture, frame and background were gilded together, at the same time, before the painter began to paint. Duccio's problem therefore was not to integrate his forms with the background but to reconcile the two. This he did by the consummate skill and elegance of his draughts-manship. His outlines are like those of the Chinese watercolour painters at their finest, suggesting great strength of form and yet doing no violence to the plane on which they are in fact painted and from which they appear to emerge.

We shall understand no more than a small part of Duccio if we regard him only as an aesthetic painter, a member of the school of art for art's sake; nor is this Madonna only an example of figurative painting as opposed to the 'abstract' painting of today. These figures were not called into existence by the artist for the sake of his picture. They had existed already for centuries in the minds of all men. They stood for charity on earth and for the hope of Heaven, embodied in the figure of a gentle and gracious super-woman who stood between the two in an attitude of intercession. It is indeed a gulf which separates this panel from a modern canvas. Those 660 years, which I began by stressing, are all there, and many more than those; for when this picture was painted the idea for which it stands, the Madonna legend, had already been the subject of pictures for a span of time as great as that which separates it from the pictures of today. Duccio is almost timeless, looking backward almost to the beginning of Christianity and yet looking forward in the Humanism which raises this picture above those of his predecessors. This is already a great example of Humanist art.

*

Siena

A city of Tuscany in central Italy, Siena is thirty-two miles south of

Florence. Crowning three hills which rise above an undulating plateau, it is largely built in brick of a soft and vivid red; but it is dominated by the black-and-white stripes of its marble-faced cathedral. The city is the seat of an archbishop, has a famous university, and is the capital of an agricultural province. Of the 60,000 inhabitants, nearly half have been added during the last twenty-five years with the development of the tourist trade; for Siena is perhaps the least spoilt of the beautiful cities of Italy and it lies on the road to Rome.

This situation, valuable when roads were few and hill-tops gave security, helped to make it exceedingly prosperous. The Sienese were bankers, above all to the Holy See. In the thirteenth and fourteenth centuries this city-state was a rival on almost equal terms with Florence, with which it was constantly at war. Its capital was one of the centres of European culture. The building and embellishment of the cathedral were the work of the leading Tuscan architects and sculptors. Nicolò Pisano and his son Giovanni came from Pisa, and spent some three years, 1266–8, building and carving; Giovanni returned later to become head of the cathedral works and sculptor of the greater part of the statues of the façade. A fragment of one of these is in the Victoria and Albert Museum. But Siena was already herself becoming the centre of a great indigenous school of painting. Guido da Siena, whose earliest surviving panel was once dated probably 1262, painted altar-pieces which were grandly monumental but did not differ fundamentally from those of other followers of the Byzantine style in Tuscany. In the last quarter of the century a distinct Sienese school was born. It remained the greatest school of Gothic painting through most of the fourteenth century and retained noble characteristics into the early Renaissance.

Biographical note

As early as 1278, Duccio di Buoninsegna was employed as painter by the Comune of Siena. It was then only a matter of the decoration of a dozen muniment chests; but such things meant more in Siena perhaps than anywhere else. Civic dignity was proud and joyous and the

25. Duccio: *Virgin and Child with Angels*, showing the triptych with its two wings closed; they are painted to resemble an inlay of precious materials

26. Duccio: *Virgin and Child with Angels*, the triptych open, showing St Dominic (left) and, probably, Sta Aurea of Ostia (right), painted on the inside of the wings; the mouldings at the edge are probably original, though restored and regilded

value of the arts in maintaining it at every level was fully understood. How he painted on the full scale in this comparatively early part of his career is not certainly known, for there is no dated picture or any which can confidently be attributed to him. But by 1285 at least his fame had already gone abroad; for he was commissioned in that

year to paint for the Rucellai Chapel in Sta Maria Novella in Florence the great altar-piece with the *Madonna and Child Enthroned, with Angels,* now in the Uffizi Gallery. It seems very probable that the stained glass of the great rose window in the fourteenth-century choir of Siena Cathedral is that which was made for a different position in 1287–8, when Giovanni Pisano was head of works, and that it was therefore actually designed by Duccio himself, as it would seem to have been. There are records again of book-covers painted by him for the Comune between 1285 and 1293, and in 1302 he was paid for a great picture of the Madonna, painted for the Chapel of the Palazzo Comunale but no longer there. It was in October 1308 that he was commissioned by the Cathedral to paint for the high altar the famous *Maestà* which was delivered and erected in June 1311. Shorn of some of the paintings from the predella (of which three are in the National Gallery), but reconstituted and recently cleaned and restored, it is now in the Cathedral Museum. Duccio died *c.* 1318–19.

The National Gallery triptych

The frames have been clumsily regilded, but otherwise the triptych is much as it was when it left Duccio's studio. The back of the large central panel is painted all over to resemble porphyry. The wings under the arch of the centre panel, which are made to fit together when the triptych is closed, are decorated on the reverse with formal patterns resembling an inlay of similar precious materials [25]. Frames and panels are all one. The piece of furniture was constructed and covered with a gesso ground, and the painter had already indicated the main outlines of his figure by incising them on the gesso when the gold leaf was applied to panels and frames and pounced with patterned borders. The haloes also seem to have been pounced with their richer patterns before the painter began to paint. We can follow Duccio's processes to a considerable extent in this picture, partly because of the clarity of his technique and partly because the wearing of the flesh painting, coupled with a tendency of all paint to become more transparent with time, enables us to see below the top layers in places. One can see in parts of the Madonna's head the sure and elegant underdrawing, and in all but the high-lights, where the paint is thickest, the green earth colour, the *terra verde*, with which he washed in the system of light and shade before the forms were fully modelled or the colours laid on. In the centre panels the uppermost pair of Angels are swinging censers [26]. In the centre of the tympanum above is King David, his name inscribed beside him (only . . .*uid* remains). Each of the other six prophets and patriarchs is identified by the words on the scroll he carries: Daniel, extreme left, with a text from Daniel ii, 45; then Moses, with a text adapted from Exodus iii, 2; then Isaiah with his invariable prophecy from vii, 14. Beyond David is Abraham, text adapted from Genesis xxii, 18, or xxvi, 4; Jacob also with a text from Genesis xxviii, 17; and Jeremiah with a text adapted from xxxi, 22. St Dominic is the subject of the left wing; this suggests that the picture was commissioned by a Dominican. Moreover, Sta Aurea of Ostia, the subject of the other wing (the remains of her name *S C A A U* ... are inscribed on the gold ground) appears in two other Sienese pictures in company with St Dominic. The triptych came to the National Gallery with the Lombardi–Baldi collection, bought in Florence in 1857. This had been brought together there by the two dealers, Francesco Lombardi and Ugo Baldi. They stated that the triptych had come from a private collection in Pisa.

Books for reference

Carli, Enzo, *Il Museo dell'Opera e la Libreria Piccolomini di Siena*, 1946, pp.34–55; *Vetrata Duccesca*, 1946

Davies, Martin, *The Earlier Italian Schools* (National Gallery Catalogue), second ed. 1961, pp.171–3

Dupont, J., and Gnudi, C., *Gothic Painting*, 1954

Guide to the Pinacoteca of Siena, 1958

The Origin of the Milky Way

Tintoretto

We do not read a painting as we do a poem, adding line to line as the eye travels along, leaving behind it memories in the mind, until we can say that we are in full possession of the poem's thoughts or its moods or the images it contains or the sequence of events it describes. Faced with a painting nothing that could be compared with the act of 'reading' takes place. You might have thought that in the presence of a narrative picture like Tintoretto's *The Origin of the Milky Way* – a picture that is primarily concerned with a 'happening' – our first impulse would be to ask: 'Who are the characters described in it? What are they doing? What dramatic situation dictates their gestures and movements?'

Sensible questions, but they can never be the first questions to ask for they all involve a time sequence. And whoever asks them and waits for the answer is throwing away the most precious gift that a great work of visual art has to offer. He is treating a painting as though it were a story – to be read. Tintoretto's picture does tell a story. But before being read it must be seen, otherwise we shall never know its real flavour. That can only be tasted at the first split-second encounter.

We are wandering through the Venetian Room in the National Gallery, unprejudiced, empty-minded, but willing to be arrested by whatever is capable of arresting us. In that mood we no more ask questions of the pictures that we meet than we question a sunrise or the view from a peak in Darien. We walk silently, and the silence is filled with sensations to which we can give only the vaguest names – words like 'serenity' or 'opulence' or 'tumult' or 'bitterness'. Those sensations occupy us like invading armies. Only when the first shock has begun to fade are we ready to ask questions like: 'Who or what is serene or opulent? And by what means are ideas about serenity and opulence communicated by the picture to me?'

We have paused in front of Tintoretto's picture. This is what I have called the 'peak-in-Darien' moment in which we ask no questions. That moment may last only for a second or two, but it is crucial.

We are conscious of two simultaneous and equally potent sensations whose names, if we can be bothered with mere words, are 'energy' and 'luminosity', or 'radiance' if you like. And it is worth noting that it is a sign of Tintoretto's personal genius that he can combine the two. For radiance one thinks of as connected with lethargy and indolent enjoyment, while energy somehow contradicts such notions. How remarkable, we think, while the picture's impact is still fresh, that any artist could have fused together such contradictory moods as indolence and movement.

The immense energy conveyed by the wildly extended limbs of the naked goddess (for we know instinctively that she is no mortal woman) and the other figure sweeping down from the sky on the right – all this is too obvious to need comment. But the radiance is more subtly achieved. Light of an unusual warmth pervades the picture – the light of midsummer playing fitfully, in disconnected flashes, on the arm, the forehead, the thighs of the woman, on the white sheet and pillow, on the flying cupids and the airborne figure, on the looped-up curtain on the left. Anything approaching darkness is confined to the lower portions of the picture where the earth lies sleeping below us. We are up in the clouds: everything is airborne. Even the bed from which our goddess has just been roused rests on layers of cloud.

But once our 'peak-in-Darien' moment has passed, it would be absurd not to ask what this picture is 'about'. Tintoretto is one of the great masters of painted narrative, and it would be both churlish and unintelligent not to listen to what he has to say. At this point it is only fair to him to tell you that the picture he painted is not quite the one that we are looking at. At some moment in the past it has been seriously amputated at the base. The sleeping earth below the clouds was once part of it. A drawing [27] in the Accademia in Venice – not a very good drawing, certainly not by Tintoretto, almost certainly not by his son, Domenico, in spite of the signature, but surely by some competent artist who had seen the picture before amputation – shows us just how much has been removed, and also how much has been left untold by the painting as we see it today.

27. Drawing after Tintoretto's *Origin of the Milky Way*, showing the full composition before the painting was cut down. Accademia, Venice

The story – it has been traced by Miss Mandowsky to its source in an old Byzantine legend – is a variant of the group of Greek myths that centre round Zeus, Heracles, and Hera. Alcmene, seduced by Zeus disguised as her husband, Amphytrion, had given birth to the infant Heracles. Zeus, anxious that his son should be given more than mortal power by being suckled by a goddess, sent his messenger Hermes with the child in his arms to the bed of Hera, his official wife. Hera, or let us call her by her Roman name, Juno, roused from her sleep by this sudden arrival, and furious with jealousy, leaps from her bed, while the milk from her breasts, exploding upwards into the sky, is transformed into the stars of the Milky Way, and falling downwards on to the earth produces a garden of lilies.

A story so confused is hardly capable of explicit translation into paint. Narrative painting, though it can build up a vivid visual account of an event, is at a disadvantage when it attempts to explain the drama behind a situation. No painting can describe intrigue or jealousy. Even Hogarth had to paint his pictures in series in order to make the plots of his stories clear, and Hogarth was an exceptionally gifted teller of stories.

Tintoretto's approach to narrative painting was more profound than Hogarth's. He, more than any other artist I can think of, went to the heart of the matter by extracting the essence of his story and translating it into purely visual language. Again and again, in his great compositions, his mind seizes on that essence. In his *Annunciation* in San Rocco, it is the wild onrush across the canvas of the Angel Gabriel with his attendants that is the real subject of the picture. In his *Bacchus and Ariadne* in the Ducal Palace in Venice it is the circle of three human figures gently revolving, like a wheel, round the joined hands of the bride and the bridegroom. In *The Origin of the Milky Way* it is, quite simply, the idea of explosion. Every line, every form, every sequence of forms, radiates wildly outwards from an maginary centre. The movement begins in the outflung arms and legs of Juno herself, roused into startled activity by the unexpected irruption of the infant Heracles. The same centrifugal force radiates outwards throughout the picture. The flying figure of Hermes – or

28. Tintoretto: preparatory drawing for *Venus and Vulcan*. Print Room, Berlin

Mercury, if we are going to use Roman names – carries us outwards (even though he is, in fact, moving inwards) to the top right-hand corner of the picture. The eye is pulled down to the bottom right-hand corner by the flying cherub and Juno's two attendant peacocks. On the left, at the bottom, another cherub drags us downwards, though this time the amputation of the picture has sliced the creature off at the waist and weakened the explosive effect. The whole axis of Juno's body leads diagonally upwards to the top left-hand corner.

You may think that to treat so human a picture as a mere diagram of the mathematics of explosion is a pedantic approach to a work of art. And so it would be if I were to say no more. Yet since Tintoretto has decided that explosion is the most effective – and indeed the only – method of telling his story, I would be doing him less than justice if I did not begin by drawing your attention to that aspect – the mathematical aspect – of the painting. But behind the mathematics lie the deeper levels which do not depend on decisions at all but which are the instinctive expressions of Tintoretto's own personal temperament. And here we come back to our 'peak-in-Darien' moment when we suddenly became conscious of this fusion of radiance and energy and began to wonder how the two could be combined without seeming to contradict each other.

Tintoretto was a Venetian, born at the very moment when Titian was at the height of his powers and when everyone in Venice regarded his genius as one that could never be surpassed. Tintoretto's earliest biographer, Carlo Ridolfi, tells us that he was sent as a pupil to Titian's studio while he was still a boy in his teens, and that Titian expelled him after ten days' tuition in a fit of jealousy. I believe Ridolfi about the expulsion. I don't believe him about the jealousy. But the vital point of the story is that the young Tintoretto found himself, at an age when everything depended on a sound studio training, 'without a master', as Ridolfi puts it.

The result was decisive. He had to invent his own methods – and very extraordinary and original they are, as Ridolfi describes them. Briefly, they were based on drawings made from smallish architectural models in which he placed wax figures made by himself and illuminated by artificial light.

The only surviving drawing of this kind is of the painting of *Venus and Vulcan* in the Munich Alte Pinakothek [28, 29]. Here we can *really* watch Tintoretto at work. (For a fuller account of his methods, see the Biographical note below.) But the point is that one could call him the first self-taught artist. And Ridolfi tells us that, once he had established himself in his own studio, he inscribed over the door a motto: 'The colour of Titian and the drawing of Michelangelo.' It is a risky motto, for artists who set out to combine the virtues of their predecessors are apt to fall between two stools – especially when the

29. Tintoretto: *Venus and Vulcan*; this finished picture, based on the drawing, shows how detail was added, the lighting modified, and mistakes corrected at a later stage. Alte Pinakothek, Munich

stools are as far apart as those of Michelangelo, the greatest of all Florentine artists, and Titian, the typical Venetian.

The Florentine School was virile, intellectual, and full of structural and muscular tensions: while Venice tended to be colourful, lyrical, sensuous, and developed a feminine ideal. To combine those two might have seemed an impossible programme, yet in this picture Tintoretto did come near to a fusion between the energy of Michelangelo and the radiance of Titian. And in doing so he produced not merely an addition of two moods but something entirely new. For what I have called a fusion is very different from an addition, just as,

123

30. Detail from Titian's *Rape of Europa*, 1559. Isabella Stewart Gardner Museum, Boston, Mass.

in the language of chemistry, there is a difference between a mechanical mixture and a chemical compound.

Take, for example, Tintoretto's attitude to the naked human body, and especially the Venetian version of the female body that had been evolved by Titian. Titian's women are conscious of their beauty and that consciousness invariably involves the notion of desirability. They ask for our admiration. The erotic overtones in a mythology by Titian, sometimes frankly stated, sometimes elusive, are always there. In Tintoretto they do not exist even when they might be appropriate.

Compare, for example, the only figure in a great Titian that has the same wild abandon as Tintoretto's Juno – the figure of Europa in the Boston picture sprawling helplessly across the back of the bull who carries her across the Hellespont [30]. She strikes us at once as beautiful and vulnerable: she is a pin-up girl. And when one thinks of all the great masters who have tackled the theme of feminine beauty, one realizes that their women somehow detach themselves from their surroundings. Rubens achieves this emphasis by a special density and texture, Renoir by a special glow, El Greco by denying its humanity, Botticelli by refusing to give it amplitude. No one but Tintoretto has taken it, emotionally, in his stride, without diminishing its importance. His Juno neither wants nor attracts our admiration. She belongs to the sun, the open air, and the wind – in fact to the Golden Age of mankind. She is as full of latent muscular power as any of Michelangelo's figures. And even though, as a conscientious scholar of Greek symbolism, Tintoretto has introduced erotic symbols – the bow and arrow of Eros, the deceptive net, the torch, the luxurious bed – yet the erotic mood is absent.

This is Tintoretto in his blithest, his most optimistic, his most frankly pagan mood. Those who know his paintings in the Scuola of San Rocco in Venice will have discovered another Tintoretto, the interpreter of New Testament tragedy, full of dark overtones, full of mystery [31]. The pagan Tintoretto can meet Titian on his own ground and sometimes outpaint him, for he has a greater mastery of the problems of space and the impact of light. The Christian Tintoretto has no rival in his own field, but outside Venice he can hardly be studied: for his tragic pictures were not superficially attractive enough to be exportable.

It is worth discussing in detail the probable date of *The Origin of the Milky Way*. Tintoretto was born in 1518, painted his first great masterpiece in 1548, and died in 1594. The picture is not documented, and it is difficult to date any particular Tintoretto on the evidence of

125

31. Detail, from Tintoretto's *Temptation of Christ,* showing Satan. Scuola Grandi di San Rocco, Venice

style, for his style did not develop with age and experience as so often happens with artists. The only internal evidence – the hair-dressing of Juno – shows that it belongs to a period when he was painting other radiant mythologies. A probable date would be 1576, when he was nearly sixty years old.

In one other important respect the painting as we see it today differs from the picture Tintoretto painted just under four hundred years ago. I have said that the Venetian School was, in general, colourful and sensuous. Tintoretto had absorbed in his youth this aspect of the Venetian tradition, and if we could see the *Milky Way* today as it was when it left Tintoretto's studio, I think it would stand out as the most opulently colourful in the whole gallery – with the possible exception of Titian's *Bacchus and Ariadne*.

Alas, time, discoloured varnish, and clumsy restoration under the varnish have dimmed its original splendour, and its restoration, though not impossible, would now be a major operation. Once it must have been a dazzling harmony of white and sunlit flesh, and one day, doubtless, it will be so again when the Gallery's restorers get round to it. Today it is still splendid but the eye has to penetrate, imaginatively, through the varnish to where the breasts of the pea-cocks glow with iridescent greens and blues and the golden light saturates the clouds. When Tintoretto reverted, as all Venetians did at one time or another, to the Golden Age of Paganism, it was Titian, not Michelangelo, who was uppermost in his heart. And here, surely, is a case where, if the picture were cleaned, we would realize that he outpainted Titian himself. Inevitably the darkened varnish on the picture's surface sets a barrier between us and the man who paint-ed it. One ought not to have to look at jewels through smoked glass.

*

Biographical note

Throughout the second half of the fifteenth century and during the whole of the sixteenth, the schools of Florence and Venice were rivals. The Venetian genius was sensuous and lyrical, with an

127

emphasis on colour rather than on line, on surface than on structure. The virility of Florence was replaced by the sensuousness of Venice. Michelangelo's ideal was the male athlete: Titian's was the desirable goddess.

When Michelangelo died in 1564, the ultimate magnificence of Florentine art died with him. When Titian died twelve years later, Venice had still not said the last word. At the very peak of Titian's career, in the mid 1540s, a young Venetian was making his first tentative experiments in the art of painting. Tintoretto, 'the little dyer' – a reference to his father's trade – was a nickname given to him early in his life. As a boy he had been taken to Titian's studio as an apprentice, but had been dismissed after ten days, according to his earliest biographer, Carlo Ridolfi. The reasons for his dismissal are not clear. Ridolfi's suggestion that the old man was jealous of the precocity of a boy still in his teens is hardly credible. Incompatibility is more likely. Titian was urbane, a man of the world, a patrician used to the company of patricians.

Tintoretto, uneducated, a *popolano*, an uncomfortable early example of the angry young man, may easily have been a disruptive influence in a well-disciplined studio.

The effect of the dismissal on Tintoretto was decisive. He was left, as Ridolfi says, 'without a master', and being a young man of immense energy and inventiveness, proceeded to devise his own methods of training himself. They included the making of small wax figures which he arranged in home-made architectural models, sometimes (if he needed airborne figures) suspending them from the ceiling, more often grouping them on the floor, but invariably lit by artificial light from above, from the front, from windows cut into the side walls, or even from below. Hundreds of preparatory drawings, made from such architectural models, must have been done, and probably destroyed once they had served their purpose. By a lucky chance one survives – the sketch [28] in Berlin for the *Venus and Vulcan* in Munich, in which nothing but the basic architectural layout and the attitudes of the figures are shown. Details were added on the finished canvas. The reflection in the circular mirror shows that an experiment with an actual mirror must have proved that Tintoretto had made a mistaken guess in the sketch. In the finished painting the reflected figure of Vulcan is reversed. The discoveries Tintoretto made by this means were surprising and often revolutionary. The interplay between space and light, the complexity of shadows cast on unexpected places and of sudden areas of equally unexpected light introduced a new kind of drama into his pictures. In addition, Tintoretto's habit of making charcoal drawings of the body in violent action at lightning speed, with what a later critic, Boschini, calls a *fulminante pennello* – a brushstroke compounded of lightning and thunder – gives to his greatest compositions a vigour and a look of improvisation that was new to the sixteenth century.

It was Tintoretto's century. Born in 1518, he died in 1594, and from the year 1548 up to the year of his death paintings of strange daring and originality poured from a busy studio, organized, in his later years, no less than that of Rubens in the following century, on factory lines. His daughter Marietta, and two of his sons, Domenico and Marco, joined the family business as soon as they were of age to help their father.

One is not surprised when Ridolfi tells us that over the door of one of the rooms in his house Tintoretto inscribed the motto – 'The colour of Titian and the drawing of Michelangelo'. Luckily Tintoretto possessed the kind of genius that could not be diluted by a motto. It is evident in all his work that what he found lacking in Titian was virility. But he had no need to borrow from Michelangelo to supply the deficiency. He had enough of his own dynamism to charge every picture he painted with a new kind of energy. In that respect he was himself; in every other respect he was a pure Venetian. He was a glutton for work and an abnormally fast worker. As a self-made artist, cut off from the usual circle of potential clients as well as from the usual routine of studio tuition, he became an unscrupulous angler for commissions, and in his maturity he acquired, by dogged persistence, two sets of clients for whom he produced what would have been, for most artists, a full lifetime's work. For the Committee of the Scuola di San Rocco, to which he was appointed official artist in 1575, he painted no less than eighty major works. They are still to be seen in the building and in the positions on walls and ceilings for which they were executed – the largest one-man exhibition in Europe. His contract with the committee was to deliver three paintings a year for the rest of his life. The pictures did, in fact, arrive at a rate that easily exceeded the timetable. For the Venetian Ducal Palace he executed with equal enthusiasm, though under less strenuous pressure, some of his most famous works, including the four superb allegories of Venice and the enormous *Paradise* whose eighty-foot span fills the width of the Hall of the Grand Council.

To compare the San Rocco pictures with those in the Ducal Palace is to realize Tintoretto's extraordinary capacity for adapting his mood to his theme. The San Rocco canvases are dark, passionate, and full of the overtones of tragedy [31]. The Ducal Palace paintings, and in particular the mythologies, are blithe, glowing, and optimistic. It was a mood Titian often attempted for it was an essentially Venetian mood. But Tintoretto's version of it was his own – more radiant, more energetic, more invaded by sun and air than in any Titian. It is in that mood of energetic, sunlit optimism that Tintoretto painted *The Origin of the Milky Way*.

History of *The Origin of the Milky Way*

The subject is taken from an old Byzantine legend which relates how the infant Hercules, carried to Juno's bed to be suckled by the goddess, so startled her that the milk from her breasts gushed forth and formed the stars of the Milky Way, and, falling on the earth below, produced a garden of lilies. It is interesting that one of Tintoretto's patrons, a certain Tomaso Rangoni of Ravenna, had as his coat of arms a device of stars and lilies, and it is possible that the picture was either commissioned by him or that he gave Tintoretto advice about the complex symbolism contained in it. More probably however it was painted for the Emperor Rudolph II. It was sold to an English collector in 1798 and passed into the collection of Lord Darnley before 1828, who sold it to the National Gallery in 1890.

Books for reference

Gould, C., *The Sixteenth-Century Venetian School* (National Gallery Catalogue), London 1959, p.89

Mandowsky, E., in the *Burlington Magazine*, vol. 72, 1938, pp.88–93

Newton, E., *Tintoretto*, 1952

Tietze, H., *Tintoretto*, 1949

The Ambassadors

Holbein

To begin with, I shall not take you to the National Gallery in Trafalgar Square, but rather further afield, both in space and time. In time, over four and a quarter centuries back: January 1534, and the paint is not yet hard on Holbein's painting known as *The Ambassadors*; he finished it perhaps less than six months ago, when the two men it portrays were in London on a diplomatic mission from France.

We have come then to a castle, a towery castle, a château called Polisy, in the north-east of France, where Burgundy borders on Champagne. It is a rich and abundant country in summer, but cold in winter, colder than in England, and the cold clings to the stone of the staircase. You are climbing up from the ground floor to the first, looking for the owner; maybe he is out, maybe everyone is out, and the only sound is your own footsteps on the stairs. You pass a window that floods the spiral with light, and then mount into semi-darkness again. Then, looking up, above you on your left, you see a shimmer of green streaked with black and red and white, and there is something in the middle of that blur. It is not yet clear, just something yellowish; it is almost as if it were trying to take shape in your eyes; you take a step on up, and you stop. The shape in the rich blur of colour above has almost hardened, and a skull hovers from the wall above you [32]. Luminous, almost phosphorescent, almost hung out from the wall like an inn-sign, only not saying welcome: a challenge, rather. But if you answer it, going on up, it dissolves in your eyes; you press on, you glance away for a second – you have reached a landing in the stairs and have to look where you are going – and when you look for the skull again, it is gone. Instead, there, almost on your own level, hangs a painting of the owner of the house, as large as life and as natural, leaning on a sort of two-tiered table that is piled with globes, musical instruments, geometrical instruments, books. At the far end of the table, leaning on it too, there is a friend of the owner.

The two men are lit by the sunlight from a window behind your

32. Detail from *The Ambassadors*; the distorted skull 'rectified', as it appears to the eye when seen from an acute angle from the right

right shoulder, and they are as vivid as birds in mating plumage against the rich green damask curtain that falls in folds behind them. The man on your left is the most striking, in a terrific luxury of clothes: basically in the most sumptuous of blacks – black hose, undercoat, and jaunty black cap, but his doublet shining pink satin, his surcoat flung back to show its lining of ermine like a foam; round his neck there is a gold chain bearing the gold medallion of the Order of St Michael; his dagger is gold and his sword hilt, and from the sling of the dagger hangs a vast tassel of gold and green. He is a very great man on earth, Jean de Dinteville by name, head of one of the most ancient and aristocratic families of France, and he presents in himself a most potent image of worldly pomp and power.

Much more subdued is his friend on your right, standing straight and almost sombre, his dark robe closed about his body. He, like the other one, is also a diplomat, but a priest as well: Georges de Selve, Bishop of Lavaur. But though his pose is grave, austere, there is little of the ascetic about him; his gown is of a noble reddish brown damask lined with a rich brown fur. And then, between the

136

33. Detail from *The Ambassadors*; the central 'still life' of instruments of learning, science, and art

sensual and physical pride of these two figures, there is the strange, crisp, almost clinical display of instruments on the table between them, all instruments for the exercise of intellect and spirit: for astronomy, arithmetic, geometry; for theology and astrology; for music [33]. The two men are young, Dinteville twenty-nine and the Bishop only twenty-five – their ages are marked on the picture – and they stand there in the splendour of their youth as though they had been selected for show as the most complete and fortunate of men; two human beings blessed with the capacity and the opportunity to extract out of life everything that it can yield. Everything of the highest order that life can yield – here there is no wine, no women, and the songs you can read in the open book are versions of the Ten Commandments and of that most triumphant of Christian hymns, *Veni creator spiritus*.

But – where has the skull gone? that skull that you glimpsed a moment ago from an oblique angle below on the stairs; which should be exactly where this lifelike, almost breathing image of the two men hangs on the wall of the landing. In fact you can see now what must be it, though as you stand square in front of the picture it has become only a meaningless streak – incoherent yet somehow sinister, like a man-eating shape refracted through depth of water. This shape sprawls diagonally, low across the foreground of the picture, and though you know what it must be, however hard you stare you cannot make it cohere with your eyes alone from where you stand. And it breaks up the monumental stillness of the painting; it does not belong there; it seems suspended between you and the two men. If you look at the faces of the men for a clue, you will not get much of an answer, though their eyes may seem a little oppressive by now – they will not let you alone. The Bishop's gaze is a little dull, opaque; Dinteville's face has a glint, an open alertness in the eyes, but the hint on the curve of the lips might be of mockery. You can look as long as you like but you will find no more open clue than that. Except, before you turn to go on up the stairs, you may spot two details you could easily miss. In the extreme top-left corner of the painting, half-hidden in the folds of the green curtain, a little

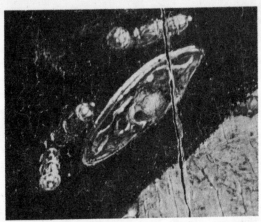

34. Detail from *The Ambassadors*; badge decorated with a skull, in Dinteville's cap

cross bearing the crucified body of Christ, a crucifix. And then – and you have to look very close to find this – in the little gold badge on Dinteville's black cap, you can just make out – again – the image of a skull [34]: like the faintest echo of the shape sprawled across the foreground played down until it is almost unnoticeable.

In the National Gallery, the seat in front of Holbein's painting of the two Ambassadors is padded and agreeably comfortable; the air is conditioned and laps you warmly with a gentle hum. The painting hangs there, one among other paintings; it is, of course, a magnificent piece of work, so skilful, so solid-seeming, the two men with the strange still life between them. And in this nuclear age, the instruments seem almost quaint in their remoteness, like Victorian bric-à-brac. There is of course that distorted skull still there, in the foreground, so strange, so curious, so clever – but perhaps really a bit too clever, spoiling the composition. In fact you may feel that I have overdone the picture, presenting it in the way I have just done. I cannot even be sure that it was meant for exactly the setting I described, though something similar seems to be the only way to answer the logical demands of the picture – it should be seen from below and from above at a very oblique angle, and also from in front, fairly close to and not much above eye-level. It is interesting, though perhaps only a coincidence, that in May 1532 – a year before this picture was painted – Dinteville was writing home about a new tower and some pictures that he was adding to his castle. *The Ambassadors* should perhaps have a dark tower all to itself – it would be worth it, for it is not simply a trick picture, a brilliant essay in deceiving the eye by the sleight of an admittedly extraordinarily skilled hand.

Let me start with the frontal view. For a portrait there is no exact parallel in its composition at this date. It has a heraldic quality that has often been commented on, I am sure rightly. In their panoply of furs and silks, the two men stand there like the two figures called in heraldry the supporters, on each side of a shield of arms. On a small scale Holbein had done many similar straight heraldic designs before – for translucent coats of arms in stained glass to hang in a window. In *The Ambassadors* there is no shield with its emblems of lineage, but instead this shop-window display of all the instruments of intellectual and spiritual accomplishment. It is almost as if these two great feudal aristocrats wished to demonstrate that aristocracy of birth and blood is not enough; aristocracy of mind and spirit is equally or even more important.

But also the composition of the two standing figures may suggest something quite other; one can read this composition as though it were a translation into secular terms of a classic religious formula of the Italian High Renaissance: that of the Virgin and Child with her saints standing on either side of her. But here the focus is not the Virgin but all those instruments that suggest the New Learning, even the Reformed Religion (the hymns are in German, in Luther's versions). You get echoes of this sort of 'secularization' of religious themes elsewhere in Holbein: in his masterpiece of his wife and children, for example, at Basle, posed like a Virgin and Child with the Infant St John the Baptist, but with his wife painted ruthlessly, all woman, and a woman of sorrows at that, innocent of divinity, an intimation of mortality. Holbein himself was a citizen of Basle, a

140

35. Holbein: *The Arms of Death*, design for his Dance of Death series, drawn in 1526 and first published in 1538. Mansell Collection, London

fiercely Protestant city, and in the year that he painted this picture in London, 1533, Henry VIII broke finally with the Church of Rome; but this cannot be pressed very far and is one of several enigmas about *The Ambassadors* still to be solved, for as far as is known both the characters who sat for this painting were staunch and orthodox Catholics. And it is the heraldic precision and symmetry of the picture that is its dominant quality – dominant, that is, until you come to the distorted skull.

But even there, in the skull, Holbein is restating a heraldic theme that he had used as frontispiece for one of his most famous works: the frontispiece to his engravings of the Dance of Death. This too was a shield of arms, with a supporter on each side, a man and a woman in the prime of their flesh; but on the shield itself, instead of the usual emblems of life rooted in the past and continuing now, there is simply a skull, and the crest is an hour-glass [35]. A theme normally used to emphasize the continuity of life has been turned inside out to show the exact opposite.

So too in *The Ambassadors*. But whereas in the Dance of Death engraving the composition is perfectly orthodox in construction at least, in *The Ambassadors* the skull utterly disrupts the orthodox rules of composing a picture. This has often been held against it, but I believe wrongly. *The Ambassadors* works perfectly well as a unity, and the critics who have objected to the skull as to a misplaced ingenuity have missed the point. For this, unlike most – indeed I think all – other single great Renaissance pictures, is not meant to be seen from one viewpoint. It is a picture in three movements, or in three acts, to see which – as in certain forms of medieval drama – the spectator and not the scenery has to move. First you see, from an oblique angle, the skull; you move forward and the skull vanishes as though it were the opening wing of a triptych to leave the central panel clear, the second act; you move on and up, and the picture is closed again with the skull.

Of course, this is also trickery; but it is much more than that. The point it makes is that the whole thing is trickery anyway; that all Renaissance painting is a trick. A basic revolution in Renaissance painting was the rediscovery of the technique of perspective, by which the illusion of a three-dimensional world could be sustained on a two-dimensional surface in a painting. And in fact the illusion of the two diplomats standing clear as life between their almost concrete instruments of learning and of art is achieved by a masterly display of the technique. But so too is the skull that seems to disrupt them: it is drawn equally strictly according to the rules of a sort of inverted or perverted perspective.

To put it another way, in spite of and because of the excellences of perspective, you cannot possibly see all the picture at once. Perspective – the pride of Renaissance artists from Van Eyck to Alberti and Leonardo, the perspective codified for northern Europe by Holbein's German forebear of the previous generation, Dürer – perspective itself is also but a vanity of vanities. Holbein himself, as indeed he shows here, was a major virtuoso of the techniques of perspective, and again and again in his works his delight in its illusionistic possibilities is obvious. Yet he was also, of all northern artists, not excepting

36 and 37. G. Stretes: *Edward VI*, 1546; a 'perspective' portrait, showing the frontal view and the 'rectified view' (as seen through a peephole from an acute angle on the right). The National Portrait Gallery, London

Dürer, the closest to the great Italians in his power of absorbing illusionistic detail into the calm and serene, the classic monumentality of the whole – as here in the figures of the two men. And all this he wilfully disrupts with a twisted skull – yet not wilfully, for the whole of this painting, the whole trinity of it, the whole paradox of subject-matter and of technique, forms an exactly calculated and profound statement of the one theme, *vanitas vanitatis*, vanity of vanities. In the midst of death we are in life, which is opened and closed by a skull. Only the crucifix, almost, as if deliberately, half-hidden in the folds of the curtain, may be construed as a half-hint of a mystery that art cannot begin to encompass: another act yet, when the green curtain will be drawn and both life and death prove to be vanities in a greater order of being known only to the vision of God.

Holbein's own personality is most elusive and opaque, but the evidence of his works is plain: he was much possessed by death, like Webster and like so many artists of the fifteenth and sixteenth centuries; yet this is not a morbid picture – it is a wry one, perhaps, but it presents its theme with extraordinary detachment in its ironic paradox, two pictures which are one and yet are not one. It has no close parallels in painting, although some other trick perspectives of the time exist [36, 37], but it can be illumined from the literature of the time, most notably Erasmus. In 1509, in Thomas More's house in London – only a little way from where Holbein was later to paint this picture – Erasmus had written one of the great books of the world – *In Praise of Folly*. Holbein of course knew Erasmus well, and in Basle had illustrated a copy of *In Praise of Folly* with pen drawings. In this there are not only passages that could almost serve as texts for Holbein's painting, where Folly claims as her own even the most accomplished of men – scientists, even theologians, and so on – but there is also a similar ironic detachment and ambiguity on the part of the author.

Much has been written about *The Ambassadors*, but there is stil much to find out. Not only details; far more, for example, needs to be discovered about the strange and splendid man, Jean de Dinteville, who commissioned it. Here I have been able to do little more than stress what I take to be its major theme, but the painting itself is there, wide open to your eyes, in the National Gallery. It may begin by baffling, and continue, still baffling, by haunting you; but of one thing I am certain, you will not come to the end of it.

*

Biographical note

Hans Holbein the Younger was born in Augsburg *c*.1497–8. By 1515 he was in Basle, Switzerland, and then in Lucerne between 1517 and 1519; he is likely also to have visited Northern Italy at this period.

From 1519 until 1526 he was solidly established in Basle. In 1526 Holbein set out for England, travelling via Antwerp. In 1528 he returned to Basle, but by 1532 was back in England; by 1536 he was employed by Henry VIII himself. In 1543 he died in London, a victim of the plague.

Jean de Dinteville and Georges de Selve

The painting known as *The Ambassadors* is the most striking set-piece remaining from the earlier part of Holbein's second English period. It is signed and dated IOANNES HOLBEIN PINGEBAT 1533. Its peculiar composition is clearly the result of close collaboration between Holbein and the man who commissioned it, and who is shown on the spectator's left: Jean de Dinteville.

Dinteville (1504–55) came of a most ancient, distinguished, and active family in the high French nobility. In mid-February 1533, he came to England on a diplomatic mission from Francis I to Henry VIII – the second, and longest, of five such visits to England; his mission was connected with the delicate and extremely tortuous manoeuvrings by which Henry VIII was trying to extract his divorce from Catherine of Aragon out of the Pope (Clement VII). Dinteville returned to France in November, doubtless taking Holbein's painting with him. His own tastes in art were obviously generous, imaginative, and somewhat recondite. There are two later portraits of him; in one of them, painted by the Dinteville private painter, Felix Chrétien, he appears as a character in a most involved representation of *Moses and Aaron before Pharaoh* (painted in 1537; now in the Metropolitan Museum, New York); in the other, painted by the leader of the Fontainebleau School, Primaticcio, he is shown as St George. He was clearly not a man who sat indifferently to any painter, and submitted.

The second figure in the picture (on the spectator's right) is Dinteville's close friend and colleague in diplomacy, Georges de Selve, Bishop of Lavaur (1508/9–41), who carried out various diplomatic missions for France in his career, and who visited Dinteville

145

38. Holbein: *Niklaus Kratzer* (Astronomer to Henry VIII), 1528; this painting shows several instruments similar to those appearing in *The Ambassadors,* for which Holbein no doubt borrowed them from Kratzer, with whom he seems to have been closely acquainted. The Louvre, Paris

in London (doubtless with business in hand) in April/May 1533, and presumably then sat to Holbein. Dinteville is twenty-nine years old; his age is inscribed on the sheath of his dagger (AET. SVAE 29). The Bishop's age is also given, on the book on which his arm rests (AETATIS SVAE 25).

39. Photograph of an actual terrestrial globe, now in the National Maritime Museum, Greenwich

40. Detail from *The Ambassadors* showing Holbein's version of a similar globe

An inventory of objects

In the extreme top-left corner a crucifix is partly hidden in the folds of the curtain.

On the top shelf of the two-tiered table or what-not, set out on a 'Turkey' carpet (carpets normally covered tables rather than floors at this time), is an array of scientific instruments. From left to right:

1. A celestial globe, showing the constellations drawn in animal form. This could be used for either astronomical or astrological purposes; the names of the constellations are inscribed in Latin, with Galicia (the Cock) in a central position; the Cock is an ancient device of France.

2. A portable ('Shepherd's') cylindrical sundial: when correctly set for date and placed facing the sun, the shadow from the style or needle at the top indicates the time. It is set here for 15 August or 11 April, presumably the latter, but is not recording a specific time; on its base three signs of the Zodiac are visible – the Ram, the Virgin, and (?) the Bull. This instrument probably belonged to Niklaus Kratzer, friend of Thomas More and astronomer to Henry VIII, and likely to have been one of Holbein's intimates in England; it appears in Holbein's portrait of Kratzer [38] in the Louvre, painted in 1528.

3. A kind of table quadrant, and behind it

4. A simple quadrant. A quadrant is an instrument for measuring angular altitudes.

5. Resting on the base of 3, an unidentified instrument with a tall vertical needle. Both 3 and 5 also appear in Kratzer's portrait in the Louvre.

6. A polyhedral sundial (also in Kratzer's portrait); the shadows cast here from the needles are inconsistent, registering about 9.30, 10.30, 10.30 respectively. It has a compass built in at the top, by which it can be set.

7. Resting on the closed book, an elaborate instrument known as Apian's Torquetum with Semissis, for determining the positions of celestial bodies. The plumbline on the pendant semicircle, or Semissis, told the altitude; here it registers between 0° and 10°.

On the lower shelf of the table, from left to right:

1. A terrestrial globe [39, 40], painted from one said to have been drawn and engraved by J. Schöner in Nuremberg in 1523. Three of these still exist, one in the National Maritime Museum. Holbein has followed this globe very closely, and most of the

names correspond; but, especially in France, names have been added, notably that of Dinteville's château, Polisy. Other added names are rather Germanized, such as Baris (for Paris), and Pritannia (for Brittany).

2. An arithmetic book, held half-open by an angle rule. This is a book by Peter Apian, *Eyn newe unnd wohlgegründte underweysung aller Kauffmanss Rechnung*, published in 1527, and here shown open at Book Three, page eight.

3. A lute, with one string broken.

4. A pair of compasses or dividers.

5. A hymn book with music, open. On the left page part of Luther's translation in German of the hymn *Veni creator spiritus*; on the right the beginning of his version of the Ten Commandments. The original book from which these were copied is not known.

6. A case of flutes.

The mosaic pavement is copied fairly closely from that in the Sanctuary at Westminster Abbey, dating from the reign of Henry III. The light in the picture falls generally evenly from above the spectator's right shoulder; the distorted skull, however, is lit at almost a right angle to the picture surface, from the right.

History of *The Ambassadors*

Originally at Dinteville's château at Polisy, it descended through his family and probably by bequests to Nicolas Beaujon; sold at his sale in Paris, 1787, it was eventually bought in England about 1809 by the Earl of Radnor, at whose house, Longford Castle, it remained until the National Gallery bought it in 1890.

Books for reference

By 1890 the work had long lost its identity, and most of what is known about it was discovered by Mary F. S. Hervey and published in her book *Holbein's 'Ambassadors'* (1900). A full and up-to-date summary is to be found in Michael Levey's entry for this painting in his *German School* (National Gallery Catalogue), 1959. There is also a very valuable chapter devoted to the picture in Jurgis Baltru-šaitis, *Anamorphoses ou perspectives curieuses* (Paris, 1955).

Note. Since writing this, an alternative, most ingenious, method of viewing *The Ambassadors* has been published by E. R. Samuel, in the *Burlington Magazine*, October 1963 (vol. CV, pp. 436–41). If the distorted skull is seen through a transparent tube about an inch in diameter (e.g. the neck of a glass vase), its drawing is rectified and the skull appears in its natural shape.

The Adoration of the Name of Jesus

El Greco

El Greco's picture *The Adoration of the Name of Jesus* or, as it is sometimes called, *The Dream of Philip II*, is a variant of a larger painting of the same subject which was done for Philip II of Spain. This larger version [41] is now in the Escorial, that strange forbidding palace built by Philip between 1562 and 1584 in the mountains thirty miles to the west of Madrid. There he lived, through all the latter part of his life, confined to his bed in a suite of minute rooms; from the bed he could overlook the high altar of the palace church, while from his study he had a clear view over the plain to his new capital of Madrid.

It was probably to the Escorial that Greco went to do his first work for the King; it was from there that he was dismissed a year or so later after painting the large and magnificent *Martyrdom of St Maurice*. This was intended for the high-altar, but it failed to please, and was demoted to a dark corner in the sacristy, where it has remained, semi-visible, ever since.

Philip's favourite painter was the fifteenth-century Fleming, Jerome, or, as he is sometimes called, Hieronymus Bosch, whose strange, fantastic medievalism and precise, minute style both seem to have had a strange appeal for him. So it is perhaps not surprising that Greco's profoundly philosophic and transcendental outlook, his wild, sweeping style, and his symbolic colouring, were less acceptable. Yet there was much about the *Adoration* that must have appealed to Philip, for the mouth of hell in the right foreground and the scene of a cave or hall with people hanging in it in the centre are both medieval in spirit and have something of the fantasy of Bosch about them.

Probably the first thing you notice about the *Adoration* in the Spanish room in the National Gallery is the way it stands out because of its colour. It has a strange, unearthly, pink glow about it, which is in some ways similar to the pink of Bosch's *Garden of Delights* that was also in Philip's possession. But the rendering and conception of

41. El Greco: *The Adoration of the Name of Jesus*; the larger version, 55⅛ by 43⅓ inches (140 by 110·1 cms.). The Escorial, Madrid

the picture are entirely different. Bosch was a narrative painter, and his work is important for its subject-matter. Greco's art is essentially interpretational, and he seeks to express the profundity of his emotions by form and colour rather than by direct representation; indeed, how else could he have treated a subject as abstract as *The Adoration of the Name of Jesus*?

Representation of a straightforward character is nevertheless there, as in all Greco's work. He could paint nature as realistically as anyone, and in our picture you will find realism in the cross at the top, or in the details of many of the figures. But the dominating emotion is ecstasy, and the profundity of his ecstatic approach is expressed in every shape, every angle, every colour relationship. In the foreground kneel two figures: the one on the left is probably the Doge of Venice in a mantle of a strange buff colour; that on the right is Philip himself, in black with a white ruff and black gloves, kneeling at a curious angle on a gold cushion. In painting his long, pale face and his strange, angular legs, Greco seems to have penetrated to the very depth of the character of this unusual individual, who ruled half the world from a bed of sickness in the Escorial. Between them, and facing the spectator, is the Pope.

Behind Philip, in the lowest plane of the picture, the great maw of hell stands open, swallowing up the damned, and ready, almost, to swallow up the spectator as well in its daring, frontal position. It is black, with huge white teeth and pink gums, and within is a mass of tortured, naked figures. Beside the Pope, facing the spectator, are two figures, the first with a white surplice and greenish-buff robe above it, the second a cardinal, in red. These perhaps represent the Cardinals Granville and Francesco de Pacheco. Behind them is a seething mass of heads, leading the way to another group, led by a strange figure in red, with arms upraised. He is perhaps Don John of Austria, Philip's half-brother. Between this group and the mouth of hell a vast hall or cave is suggested rather than depicted, with figures in grey on what is apparently a bridge, almost silhouetted against the purple, pink, and red flames behind the mouth of hell itself, and with figures apparently hanging within it; it is another

42. Detail from *The Last Judgement*, Byzantine painting of the 'Cretan' School. Mount Athos, Monastery of the Lavra

instance of medieval symbolism, the bridge being the passage to purgatory, which the good pass over while the wicked fall into the abyss.

At the top of the picture the Jesuit emblem, in the form of the letters IHS with a cross rising from the horizontal bar of the H, stands out against the traditional medieval *mandorla* or brilliance of glory, the colour of the pale sun of an early midsummer morning. Crowds of angels are around, in adoration, and they and the clouds on which they are poised seem to reflect an unworldly glow of heavenly brilliance, which is made the more striking by the heavy grey of the clouds on either side; these would seem ominous if they did not serve to intensify the glory of the central composition, and if they were not offset by the brilliant purple-red robes of two of the angels that rest on them on either side. Below the cloud, to the spectator's left, the buff and the green robes and parts of the legs of two other angels are seen, their bodies wholly obscured by the cloud – who but Greco would have dared to paint them like that?

At the bottom left-hand corner is an inscription in Greek, '*Domenicos Theotocopoulos Kres epoie*' – Domenicos Theotocopoulos the Cretan did it.

The whole conception of the picture is strange and unexpected. The colouring is forceful, daring, and unusual, and it is a brilliant piece of painting, which would be at home beside the work of a Chagall or a Graham Sutherland today. But surpassing that in many modern works is the sense of form, as well as the way in which the figures are painted. Their great, muscular arms and 'olympic' legs reflect the works of Michelangelo, and form a curious contrast with the puny yet characterful figure of Philip.

There has been a good deal of discussion about the reasons why the picture was painted. The Jesuits were powerful, and the theme of *The Adoration of the Name of Jesus* was normal enough. But why hell below, and why the figures of the Pope, Philip, and the Doge of Venice? Professor Sir Anthony Blunt, in a study of the Escorial version of this picture, proposes that it was done to commemorate the Triple Alliance of Spain, Venice, and Rome against the Turks

43. El Greco: *View of Toledo*. Casa Greco, Toledo

which culminated in the Battle of Lepanto in 1571. This explains
the three figures. It would also explain the presence of Don John,
the victor of the battle. The cross and the symbol IHS would
signalize the victory, and at the same time attest the triumph of
Christendom. Hell is there to call to mind the fate awaiting the
infidel, and the Glorification above attributes the victory to divine
providence.

This is a probable explanation, and no one surely would wish to
dispute it today. But the basic conception of the composition of the
Adoration – and this is true both of the Escorial and of the National
Gallery versions – has a rather different origin; it must have been
suggested to Greco by the common medieval theme of the Last
Judgement. Details, such as the mouth of hell and the choirs of
angels, the Holy Men and the Holy Women, were taken almost
directly from the medieval world, where the theme of the Last
Judgement was a usual one.

This was so not only in Gothic, but also in Romanesque and later

44. Byzantine School: *The Nativity,* wall painting. Mount Athos, Monastery of the Xenophontos

45. El Greco: *View of Mount Sinai*; this is probably one of the first pictures painted by Greco after his arrival in Italy. Galleria Estense, Modena

Byzantine art. There is a rendering [42] in the refectory of the Monastery of the Lavra on Mount Athos in Greece which is very similar in its arrangement, though the mouth of hell is there set sideways; its frontal position in the *Adoration* serves to attest Greco's greater skill and daring. The Lavra painting is a work of the so-called Cretan school of Byzantine art, and wall paintings that were very like it were no doubt seen by Greco in his native island of Crete when he lived there as a youth before he went to Venice.

Similarly, though less obviously, the unnaturally obtuse angle of Philip's knees, and the position of his hands, go back to Byzantine prototypes. The habit of poising angels on clouds was also usual in Byzantine art. It is true that angels on clouds appear often enough elsewhere, but only in Byzantine art do we see just the same curious framing of a single group on a single cloud. The treatment seems at the same time to attest the other-worldly character of the figures and to make them a vital part of the composition.

Greco, incidentally, made use of clouds in the same way on more than one occasion; for instance, in one of his views of Toledo, which is now in that city, the Tavera Hospital has been wafted on a cloud from its natural setting, where it was not visible from the painter's standpoint, to a place in the foreground of the painting, where it plays a prominent part in the picture [43].

Mannerisms like this have often been considered, wrongly, as Greco's personal idiosyncrasies. The real explanation is to be found in the painter's Byzantine background. For Byzantine art, indeed the whole of Byzantine thought, was governed by an unworldly, transcendental outlook, and a dominating belief in the miraculous.

Man was there, on earth, and his form provided the subject-matter of art. But art was not to the Byzantine mind bound by earthly considerations, for it sought to escape them and express the infinite. When Goldscheider wrote about *The Adoration of the Name of Jesus* just before the war he said: 'This picture can only be understood as a reflection of the shadowy light, the iridescent colour, the incoherent flash of details and the convincing improbabilities of a dream.' But there are hundreds of similar instances in the story of Byzantine art where dreams had no part to play at all. Goldscheider was surely forgetting that Greco had been nourished not in a western but in an eastern tradition. It is there that part at least of Greco's heritage is to be found – there too the strange elongated figures which he so favoured appeared time and time again throughout the centuries.

There is virtually no Byzantine painting on a large scale to be seen in this country, but the miniatures used to decorate the manuscripts of the Gospels in the British Museum or the Bodleian Library at Oxford serve to give some idea, and if you look at a reproduction of any Byzantine Nativity [44] you will be able to trace the same unworldly colouring, the same outlook, and often the same iconography that is evident in Greco, though the style of the work is of course distinct.

Many others have failed to appreciate that Greco's work had a long line of predecessors so far as iconography and understanding were concerned. This is true of Paul Guinard, when he says that the Sinai landscape, which forms a part of the lovely triptych by Greco now at Modena [45], 'answers to a fantastic or anyhow surreal conception of landscape'. The painting is the forerunner of much that we see in the works of many of our present-day painters. But it also follows an age-old tradition in Byzantine art – as we see it in renderings of the Transfiguration scene – to which Greco turned when he painted the triptych, presumably soon after his arrival in Italy.

Artists have, throughout the ages, always borrowed from the past. The study of art is not concerned with isolated manifestations, however brilliant, but rather with a series of interlinked developments, though the links vary in shape and size, sometimes being numerous and short, sometimes large and embracing lengthy periods. There are links that bind Greco to Italy, and he learnt much from Tintoretto, Bassano, and Titian. There are links that bind him to Michelangelo, whose work he must have seen in Rome (though he did not admire it – 'a nice man, Michelangelo,' he said, 'but he can't paint'). But, of all the links, that which binds Greco to the

Byzantine world is probably the most important, and it seems to have acted with renewed force when once he had become established in Spain. The strange formal shapes of mountains or clouds, the setting of figures against a sort of foil or reflex, the posing of figures as if levitated, are all Byzantine mannerisms, and many of the actual compositions follow Byzantine iconographical prototypes. And his habit of signing in Greek script with the special formula 'Domenicos the Cretan did it' was again derived from one usual among Greek icon painters of the age. Indeed, the very essence of his being was Byzantine, though in his personal genius he stepped right outside the Byzantine frame.

What of his influence on the painters that followed? What heritage did Greco leave? Velázquez, in some of his work, undoubtedly owed a great debt to him, and the link is obvious, but it was not lasting; Velázquez – when he found himself, or rather, perhaps, when his role was finally cast for him, in the court of Philip IV – changed to a more mundane and matter-of-fact approach. But then there was a gap – for it was not until the twentieth century that what may be termed 'interpretational painting' began to be lived once more, and men like Gauguin and Cézanne, Chagall or Graham Sutherland took it up where Greco had left it. These men, and others, were to become the great masters of interpretation, as opposed to Rembrandt or Reynolds, Claude or Constable, who were still essentially masters of representation.

To explain what I mean by this term 'interpretation', I cannot do better than to quote a passage from a book in which I was associated a good many years ago, with my friend Robert Byron, a great critic and a fine writer, who, 'pondering his writer's ambitions as he walked the encircling hills of Toledo', wrote that he:

suddenly knew that Greco had taught him as no other man had ever done, what can be made of the symbols of human understanding. The instruments of language and colour, of grammar and brush, became suddenly inseparable. Only the purpose of art was apparent – to express through beauty the purpose of man. It seemed for one transient

163

moment as though not only any artist, but any human being whatsoever, engaged in any high aim, might model his work on Greco's. The illusion passed. But there remained a new and deeper knowledge of that single quest which is at the bottom of all true art and thought.

Greco is not an easy artist to understand. He forsook pure naturalism; he made use of strange, imaginative shapes and of even stranger colouring. His art depended little on representation, and the proportions of his figures were not of this world. There is a visionary quality, an other-worldly beauty, and a strange profundity about his pictures that is rare to find. *The Adoration of the Name of Jesus*, perhaps more than any of his works, sets him apart from his contemporaries. It represents the quintessence of his style. Our version in London may be smaller than that at the Escorial, but it is no less brilliant. It is one of our great national treasures, and we are lucky to have it.

*

El Greco and his reputation

In the last century Greco's merits as a painter were wholly disregarded. In 1860, the entry on El Greco in Murray's *Guide to Spain* says that his colouring was ashy-grey and monotonous and his drawing execrable, and adds that these defects rendered his pictures singularly disagreeable. In 1899 he was referred to in *Chambers's Encyclopaedia* as the man 'who painted horrors in the Escorial'. In view of this it is not surprising that there had not been much in the way of serious inquiry into his history and his origin; or indeed, into the nature of his work. Any appreciation of him as a painter of outstandingly lovely and moving pictures indeed can hardly be said to have preceded the publication of Cossio's great analytical work in 1908.

It certainly did not become general on the Continent till the publication of Meier Graefe's *Spanische Reise* a few years later; and it was to a great extent thanks to the translation of this book into English and its publication in that language in 1926 that Greco began to be appreciated in this country outside a somewhat narrow circle. Meier Graefe, one of the most outstanding critics of the day, who had done more to bring about the recognition of the later Impressionists than any other writer, went to Spain in those easy days before the First World War with the idea of learning more at first hand about one of the idols of the day, Velázquez. Arrived in Spain he discovered El Greco, and the first objective of his journey was forgotten. Instead he brought into recognition the painter of the past whose work probably meant more than that of any other man to the thought and outlook of the second quarter of the twentieth century.

But even if Greco's genius had been recognized, his heritage was still obscure, and all sorts of attempts were made to prove that he was an eccentric, that he suffered from defective eyesight, or that he was perverse in his visual attitude. It was not until the early twenties that attention began to be turned to his origins. 'Domenicos Theotocopoulos the Cretan' he liked to sign himself, and the signatures had always been clear and obvious. But only then did Bertaux in France and Sir Charles Holmes in Britain look towards his native land with a view to inquiring what was going on there when Greco was a young man. Once it had begun, the inquiry was avidly pursued; in 1930 my friend Robert Byron and I produced a book called *The Birth of Western Painting*, which was designed to stress the quality of later Byzantine painting and to show how the masters responsible for wall paintings in what were then obscure churches in the East Christian world were in many ways the precursors of much that was revered in the west and, not the least, of Greco; only by taking these Byzantine works into account could many things which seemed in Greco strange and inexplicable fall into their proper place and due order.

Greco went from Crete to Venice in about 1571, and from Venice to Spain in 1577. He appears to have gone at once to Toledo, and except for a brief excursion to Madrid, when the *Adoration* was painted, it was there that he spent the rest of his life. From the first he was successful, and he was paid high prices; thus he received 1,200 ducats for the *Burial of Count Orgas* which amounts to about £2,000 of our money today. He died in Toledo in 1614.

History of *The Adoration of the Name of Jesus*

The National Gallery painting of *The Adoration of the Name of Jesus*, which measures 21⅜ by 14 inches (54·2 by 35·6 cms.), is to be identified with a picture listed in the inventory of Don Gaspar de Haro, Marqés de Helice, where it formed a pendant to a small version of Greco's *Espolio*, now in Lord Bearsted's Collection at Upton House. It may have passed from there to the Duke of Alba's collection, where it remained till *c*.1802. In 1836 it was in the Galerie Espagnole at the Louvre, and was bought for Sir William Stirling Maxwell at Louis Philippe's sale in 1853; it was bought by the National Gallery in 1955. There is a similar, but much larger version, in the Escorial, which measures 55⅛ by 43⅜ inches (140 by 110·1 cms.). The National Gallery picture is thus not only smaller than the one in the Escorial, but is also taller and narrower in proportion. The three principal figures below are closer together in the London version, and the ground behind is arranged in a different and, it must be admitted, a less satisfactory manner, and there is again less coherence and solidity of form in the middle register. But its tall, thin proportions lend to the National Gallery picture a more transcendent atmosphere and are in closer keeping both with the theme of the picture and with Greco's ideas as a whole.

There has been some dissension among the authorities as to the date of the panels. Most writers date the Escorial painting to *c*.1579 and regard the National Gallery one as later, dating it 1580–82. Professor Blunt supports this dating with the suggestion that the picture recorded the triple alliance between Rome, Venice, and Spain against the Turks; one of the figures behind the Pope probably represents Don John of Austria, who was high-admiral at Lepanto, and the picture, he thinks, was intended to hang above Don John's tomb in the Escorial, where he was buried in 1579.

One man, Camon Aznar, suggests that the London version was an earlier trial piece, while the oldest authority, Cossio, dates the Escorial picture to around 1600, saying that its fantasy accords better with Greco's later than with his earlier manner with regard to both colouring and composition. His suggestion is however not in accord with an older theory that Greco did at least one, if not both, of these paintings soon after his arrival in Spain, and that it was on the strength of this that he was given the commission for the large *St Maurice* in the Escorial, which was done between 1580 and 1584. Nor does it accord with what we now know of the development of Greco's style – much of it knowledge accumulated since Cossio wrote his book in 1908.

On balance the most probable sequence for these pictures would seem to be, first, the Escorial *Adoration* done about 1579; second, the *Martyrdom of St Maurice* commissioned on the strength of the first version of the *Adoration* and painted between 1580 and 1584; and third, the National Gallery painting of the *Adoration*, done as a second version of the first, probably while work on the *St Maurice* was still in progress.

Books for reference

Aznar, Camon, *Domenico Greco*, Madrid, 1950

Blunt, A., 'El Greco's Dream of Philip II; an allegory of the Holy League', in the *Journal of the Warburg Institute*, III, 1939–40

Byron, R., and Rice, D. Talbot, *The Birth of Western Painting*, 1930

Cossio, M., *El Greco*, Madrid, 1908; *Domenico Theotocopuli: El Greco*, 1955

Goldscheider, L., *El Greco*, third ed., 1954

Guinard, P., *El Greco*, 1956

Legendre, M., and Hartmann, A., *El Greco*, Paris, 1937

Rutter, F., *El Greco, 1541–1614*, 1930

Vallentin, A., *El Greco*, 1954

The Triumph of Caesar

Mantegna

If you go to Hampton Court in winter, as I did in February, you will find a greenish-dark, haunted world of silence broken only by the sound of birds and the scrunching of your own footsteps on the gravel. The great empty paths stretch away into space, cutting across the frosty lawns. The gardens are deserted. A smoky white light hovers under the dark trees. Sometimes a pale sculpture can be seen in a clearing, half-hidden by dim shrubberies. The fountains are empty and wait for spring before their jets can be heard and seen. Heavily ornamental urns loom up on terraces and emphasize only the desolate spaces of the long walks and promenades which lie vacant under a cold winter sun.

The massive Wren building, so richly embellished with its glowing pink-orange brick and grey stonework, seems to protect or hide the sprawling Tudor remains like a guilty secret. Elizabeth Bowen, the writer, or Michael Andrews, the painter, would I think recognize the strange atmosphere of winter at Hampton Court. The emptiness, and the light, and the nearness of the winter river give out these sensations; but you almost expect to come across something strange or unfamiliar over a hedge. You are not quite sure whether somebody is working in a greenhouse or not. The place is heavy with silence.

In summer, the terraces are crowded, the flower beds blaze with colour, the fountains play, people sprawl on the lawns and wander in throngs through the courtyards and corridors of the palace. But Hampton Court is not easily invaded by people; it retains very much its own presence. It gives out an implacable sense of separateness: of being the tomb of a family who had little to do with the rest of life. And under that bristling forest of chimney stacks is housed Mantegna's *The Triumph of Caesar*, in the Orangery, in a garden house, next door to where you pay a few pence to see an old boa-constrictor of a vine growing improbably under English glass. It costs threepence to go next door and see *The Triumph of Caesar*.

I can think of no more bizarre setting for Mantegna's masterpiece.

Carefully lettered signposts point the way 'to the Mantegna paintings' from several directions in the gardens. When you finally enter the Orangery it is like going into the reptile house at some amiable, quiet zoo. Once inside the long, single-storeyed building the illusion of a reptile house gives place to an aquarium, heightened by the way the paintings are faced by windows covered with slatted blinds. Soft under-water light filters through these blinds, reinforced by strip lighting which points up at the paintings from a low wall three or four feet away from them: a sturdy barrier, rather like that cautious division between you and the reptile tanks or cages.

What are these paintings doing in England, in the Orangery at Hampton Court? They do not burst upon you as they should, for you see them sideways. There is time to consider their presence and their origins. They were bought by Charles I from the Gonzaga family in Italy, in the early years of the seventeenth century. The Gonzagas had been Mantegna's lifelong patrons, but their fortunes were spent, and so the Mantegnas came to England. The Raphael cartoons in the Victoria and Albert Museum were also bought by that uniquely discerning monarch Charles I, but whereas the Raphaels are most nobly displayed, the great Mantegna paintings are, I feel strongly, betrayed by their present position.

If Mantegna could see his *Triumph of Caesar* now, he would scarcely recognize it, for it has suffered greatly in the past four hundred years – and it was in far from perfect condition when it first came to England. But Mantegna might well bring a case against the English for the way it is hung, which destroys the point of the paintings – for Mantegna was frequently an irascible man and entered into many legal actions in his lifetime.*

He was born in 1431, in Italy, the son of a carpenter. He was

*Since the above was written, necessarily cautious, but rewarding, beginnings at cleaning and restoration have been undertaken and are to be pursued. The siting and arrangement of the paintings are also being reconsidered. Those interested will find an interim report on the problems and progress in the *Burlington Magazine*, August 1962 [Editor].

apprenticed in Padua to a copyist and purveyor of antiques. Living and working in northern Italy, as he did, Mantegna came under the influence of Florentine art with its concentrated intellectual bite and all its compressed energy. In much of Mantegna's work we are conscious of an almost authoritarian harshness of attack. He was much affected by the sculpture of Donatello, and was in fact temperamentally drawn towards an almost sculptural firmness of modelling in his own paintings. In later years he even painted in the manner of sculptural, three-dimensional, bas-reliefs. But Mantegna was taken to Venice when he was still a young man, and met the Bellini family. He married old Jacopo Bellini's daughter; and was affected by the richer and more obviously sensual style of Venetian art in general. In Mantegna's best work the north and the south came together most beautifully, a perfect fusion between intellect and emotion: between thought and feeling. And we find this extraordinary synthesis most perfectly attained in *The Triumph of Caesar*.

Mantegna had left Padua, a centre of learning and scholarship which appealed to his imagination as a place of residence because of his own sympathy towards learning and humanism – and the current passion for antiquity – very reluctantly to enter the services of the Marquess of Mantua, Lodovico Gonzaga. He was employed by the Gonzaga family for the rest of his life as their honoured and cherished court painter; and Mantegna painted *The Triumph of Caesar* for the grandson of the Marquess, Giovanni Francesco Gonzaga, who had married Isabella d'Este.

The nine paintings in tempera on fine linen took nearly ten years to complete. They were interrupted by a visit to Rome – one of several made by Mantegna. Each mural-sized painting measures roughly nine feet square. They were first used as a decoration for an outer courtyard, and then also as a decoration for a theatrical spectacle. But just before Mantegna died the paintings were properly sited and projected at a new palace built by Francesco Gonzaga. There they probably remained until the decline of the Gonzaga fortunes, when Charles I bought them for England.

What are the paintings about? A crowded, tumultuous procession heralds the arrival of Caesar, the victor, the conqueror. Caesar in his chariot is the last painting, on the extreme right, and everything reads back gradually to him; though you can read the paintings from right to left or vice versa – the composition is a study in crescendo, either way.

First, we see the trumpeters heralding the arrival of the procession [46]. Then soldiers appear carrying statues of the gods and a tablet proclaiming Caesar's triumph [47]; a triumphal car and bier laden with the spoils of war [48]; the vase bearers [49]; sacrificial bulls followed by four richly ornamented elephants [50]; the victorious soldiers again [51], followed by the captives [52]; and finally the musicians [53], followed by Caesar in his chariot [see colour plate].

The paintings were originally in brilliant colours, but now they have faded – and have been tampered with – and so all we see is a range of soft browns and golds, enlivened by an occasional flash of light red, with a little yellow, green, and blue. An undulating land-scape binds several of the paintings together, and the long crowded composition is unified by other means as well: both in construction and balance of forms and by certain figures which pass out of one painting and enter into the next. The first three paintings push heavily to the left – the weight of the composition runs diagonally across, and upwards, building up always to the left; and this accentu-ates the effect of a moving procession surging along to the left. But the fourth and fifth paintings, the vase bearers and the elephants, bring in heavily scored conflicting diagonals and so we are led back to the right, back to the culminating-point or the beginning of the whole movement – Caesar himself.

This is probably an apocryphal triumph, for although Mantegna loved Rome he liked to embody his dream in a reinterpretation of the classical heritage. He had a highly romantic sense of the past. But the scene is Rome, for triumphs always took place in that city and this might represent the end of the Gallic wars.

Over the procession is the light of late afternoon, though the faded and altered state of the colour makes it hard to be certain. The

46. *The Triumph of Caesar*: The Standard Bearers

47. *The Triumph of Caesar*: The Triumphal Car

48. *The Triumph of Caesar*: The Litter Bearers

49. *The Triumph of Caesar*: The Vase Bearers

50. *The Triumph of Caesar*: The Elephants

51. *The Triumph of Caesar*: The Corslet Bearers

52. *The Triumph of Caesar*: The Captives

53. *The Triumph of Caesar*: The Musicians

paintings are full of the interaction between people, animals, and objects – lances, spears, caskets, and so on – and people with each other. There are marvellous details of faces peering between other bodies and the thrust and the shape of a sword or the swirling draperies of a robe which touch upon another figure and so bring that figure into the continuous interplay of the composition as a whole. Occasionally, a young soldier, a musician, or a captive looks back towards Caesar, and by this gesture the flowing composition is momentarily slowed down and our eyes pause, our intelligences are given a rest, momentarily, before the movement picks up again and swirls on. There is a tremendous tension between the long flowing horizontals and the exultant upthrust of trumpets, banners, and trophies. There is a complexity in the hectic nature of the design and in its calmly resolved execution which brings to mind Uccello's *Rout of San Romano*.

But Mantegna's vision of Caesar's triumphal procession really bears about as much relation to ancient Rome as Dukas' ballet *La Péri*, with all its *art nouveau*, *opéra comique* undertones, does to the original Persian legend which inspired it. *The Triumph of Caesar* is very much Mantegna's triumph, for he had come through to a softer and more voluptuous conception of figures than most of his other work would indicate – Venetian art had at last penetrated deeply – but the painting as a whole is like a balletic frieze, monumentally theatrical, remote from reality, a dressed-up, impeccably costumed pageant. There is real feeling in the faces and gestures of the prisoners, and much lyrical tenderness in the posture of several more contemplative figures, but most of all we are conscious of a great spectacle which re-enacts an occasion, not the occasion itself.

For thoughts of ancient Rome at the time of the Renaissance were of this order: the Italians of the Renaissance looked back upon an exotic and fabulous past, already a little hazy. Mantegna, a great humanist with a real love for antiquity, had always been fascinated by thoughts of the imperial might and majesty of Rome. You can find this predilection for weighty and heavily materialist volumes and masses even in his *The Agony in the Garden* in the National Gallery

54. Mantegna: *The Agony in the Garden*, c. 1450. The National Gallery, London

[54], where the rigid contours of the rocks and the sculptural contours of the landscape are not unlike the oppressive, heavy grandeur of Roman architecture. By contrast, Donatello went further back, imaginatively, in his reconstruction of a romantic past – and touched upon Greece. This is clear enough in the purity of his sculptures.

But Mantegna had no wish to go further back than Rome, where the Greek spirit had already become corrupted. His work perhaps is not quite spiritual enough as a result: think for a moment of his relatives, the Bellinis. And yet, although there are so many signs of

Mantegna's love of classical props and references in the paintings at Hampton Court, these are real people, not characters. A psychological penetration in the faces almost recalls the spirit of Masaccio.

It is wonderful to find *The Triumph of Caesar* as a work of Mantegna's maturity, after the pain and fierceness of most of his other paintings. Hemingway once referred to 'the bitter nail holes of Mantegna's *Christ*' [55].* But with Caesar the harshness has disappeared. The construction is firm enough, but the work as a whole is a gentle, calm evocation of the classical world. The conception itself is highly original, for the figures are all on a low ground so that they would appear to be moving at eye-level. This illusion of reality would be greatly heightened by implementing Mantegna's original plan for placing the separated panels between thin carved pillars which make a fixed, *ideal* plane – so that the procession would seem to take place on the other side of the pillars.

At Hampton Court the paintings are placed high above eye-level and they are separated by spaces, without pillars. The white striplights from below illuminate only the centre parts of each painting. A pool of shadow obscures the base of each composition. Mantegna's conception of a unified procession is completely destroyed. It would be startling to see these paintings at eye-level, properly illuminated and recessed by pillars according to Mantegna's plan. Worst of all, perhaps, is the impossibility of getting far enough away from the paintings to see the work as a whole, for they hang along one side of a long narrow gallery. Mantegna did not want us to have the impression of a set of framed pictures, with the frames confusingly at the same plane as the action.

But it is still a great experience to see this extraordinary vision unroll before our eyes. Hanging in the room where I write at home is a painting of Buddha in his chariot that I brought back from Siam recently. It is old, with soft colours and gilding on frayed linen; but

*This is as quoted by Aldous Huxley in *Music at Night*; later Hemingway (in *Death in the Afternoon*, 1932, pp.181–3) said that he had been unable to find the quote in his work, but for what he did in fact write see *A Farewell to Arms*, chap. 37 [Editor].

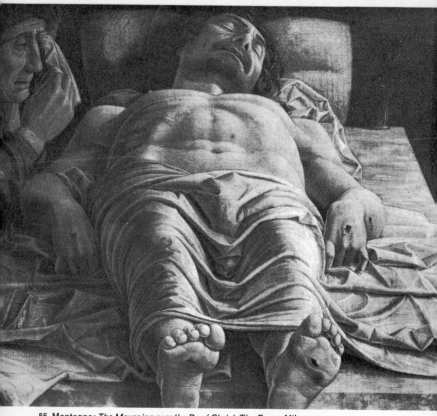

55. Mantegna: *The Mourning over the Dead Christ.* The Brera, Milan

there is immense charm and vivacity in the painting of the handsome young Prince who was to become Buddha by divesting himself of his riches: setting out on the first stage of his journey towards the real life of the spirit and leaning over his chariot to give alms to the four seated beggars by the roadside. I would rather think of Buddha than of Caesar; but Mantegna touched upon an almost oriental conception of painting and a sweet compassion of colour and gentle modelling in this *Triumph* that Buddha might well have smiled upon.

*

Andrea Mantegna was born in 1431 at Isola di Cartura, near Piazzola. He was the son of a carpenter, and apprenticed at the age of ten to Squarcione, a copyist and purveyor of antiques, at his workshop in Padua; with other apprentices, Mantegna became his adopted son. At seventeen, he left his master and established himself independently in Padua. Just before this he stayed for a short time in Venice with Squarcione and probably met for the first time Jacopo Bellini and his two sons, Giovanni and Gentile.

In 1448 Mantegna received the commission for the decorations, devoted to SS. James and Christopher, in the Ovetari Chapel of the Eremitari church at Padua. (These, and earlier decorations for another church, representing his first commission, have been destroyed – except for *The Martyrdom of St Christopher* and *The Assumption of the Virgin* in the Eremitari church.) Other commissions followed, and in *c*.1453 Mantegna married Nicolosia, the daughter of Jacopo Bellini, thus becoming brother-in-law to the two famous sons.

In 1459 he entered the service of Lodovico Gonzaga, Marquis of Mantua, as Court painter, and remained as official artist to the Gonzaga family for the rest of his life. After leaving Padua he lived almost continuously at Mantua, with many commissions to fulfil in connexion with Court festivities and pageants. These included decorations and portraits of the Gonzaga family for the palace and its chapel, as well as *The Triumph of Caesar*. He also produced a small number of works which are independent of Court commissions.

After the death of Lodovico Gonzaga, Mantegna was employed by his son, Federico, and very shortly after this by the grandson, Giovanni: his position in the Gonzaga household was both intimate and honoured.

Mantegna's last works were executed for Isabella d'Este (who married Giovanni Gonzaga), mainly for her salon at the Gonzaga palace which also contained paintings by other artists. The contents of this salon are now in the Louvre.

Mantegna died in 1506. Nearly all his principal works in chapels and palaces have been lost or destroyed; the few that survive are in deplorable condition with few remaining traces of Mantegna's hand; many isolated works in public collections in Europe and the U.S.A. have, with few exceptions, been greatly restored and re-touched.

History of *The Triumph of Caesar*

The nine paintings in tempera on fine linen each measure approximately 107 by 112 inches. They were painted for Giovanni Francesco Gonzaga, between 1485 and 1494. First used as a decoration for an outer courtyard at the Gonzaga palace, they were later employed as a decoration at a theatrical spectacle. Just before the artist's death, they were placed in the new palace built by Francesco Gonzaga at the Porta Pusterla. There, the paintings were properly shown, doubtless according to Mantegna's original conception, through being divided by painted pilasters. In this way, the long procession seen from eye-level moves from right to left and would appear to be recessed by the pilasters, thus accentuating the elaborately devised realist perspective of the paintings as a whole. Eventually, however, the *Triumph* was returned to the Ducal Palace. Following the dis-solution of the Gonzaga fortunes in the early part of the seventeenth century, the paintings were purchased by Charles I and placed at once at Hampton Court.

In sequence from left to right, the paintings depict:

1. The trumpeters and standard bearers showing the painted scenes of battles;
2. Statues of the gods, the spoils of wars, a triumphal car, and the tablet proclaiming Caesar's Triumph;
3. A triumphal car and bier laden with other spoils;
4. Figures and animals in procession to the sacrifice;
5. Sacrificial bulls followed by four richly ornamented elephants;
6. Victorious soldiers;
7. The captives;

8. Musicians and standard bearers;

9. Caesar on his triumphal car, with Roma turning back towards the victor.

Exposure to the elements and bad conservation before even the early years of English ownership, destructive cleaning, and later inept and over-zealous restoration have left us only a faint, and in many parts extremely crude, approximation to Mantegna's original conception. Even so, its splendour comes through to us if we are patient.

In *The Triumph of Caesar*, which may well be considered Mantegna's masterpiece, we find all the ingredients of an event containing the props and symbols of classical Roman antiquity but expressed in an altogether softer and less harsh manner. The mood of *The Agony in the Garden* or the *Dead Christ* [55] has shifted. The influence underlying *The Triumph* comes more from Venice than from Florence. Mantegna had already discovered that the Venetians substituted painting on canvas for fresco, because of climate, and saw the possibilities of painting on a very fine canvas or linen with scarcely perceptible washes of thin tempera. This made possible a more subtle modulation of tones, otherwise impossible with tempera. Light and shade and modelling are reduced to the minimum necessary for the construction of figures. The approach in general is not dissimilar to the distillation of modelling and tonality that we find in Chinese art. *The Triumph* is quite free of the acerbity of line and somewhat theatrical sharpness of modelling that distinguish the greater number of Mantegna's works, though the structure of the paintings, with their inventive interplay between shifting horizontals and exultant verticals, is exceedingly dramatic.

In this great work the linear energy of the Florentines is combined at last with an affection for Venetian art but still animated by an intellect formed at Padua, where Donatello had also influenced the style of Mantegna.

Books for reference

Berenson, Bernard, *Italian Painters of the Renaissance*, 1952
Millar, Oliver, *The Triumph of Julius Caesar*, 1960
Tietze-Conrat, E., *Mantegna*, 1952

The Entertainment

Hogarth

Hogarth's fame, his popularity, and his income derived largely from the sale of prints – prints from engraved plates which he either engraved himself or got professionals to do for him. Some of these prints – the 'Industry and Idleness' series, for instance – were based on drawings, but the more important series came from highly finished oil-paintings, and that of course, is the case with 'The Election'. The first of the four – *The Entertainment* – was engraved by Hogarth himself and he tried to finish it without taking a single proof. The thing went wrong. Hogarth stamped, roared, and swore he was ruined, and some kind friends had to come in and calm him down and correct the blunders. The resulting engraving is a vigorous but singularly unflattering interpretation of the painting: the other three 'Election' engravings were finished by professionals.

It was these engravings which declared Hogarth to the world, made people laugh and moralize and wonder at his genius. The original paintings remained in his studio. The 'Election' series – four big paintings – should have represented a valuable asset but for some reason nobody seemed to want them and they hung about, priced rather modestly at 200 guineas. Eventually, Hogarth decided to raffle them. He called on Garrick, the actor, and asked him to head the subscription list. Garrick said he would come and see the pictures; which he did, and duly subscribed. Then, just as he was leaving Hogarth's house, a humiliating thought struck him. Here was Hogarth, an old friend, not rich, wanting just fifty guineas apiece for four great pictures. And here was Garrick, the affluent actor, idol of the public, obliging his friend to the extent of patronizing a lottery. It was hardly in character. He went straight back and bought the pictures.

They went to his villa at Hampton, and I suppose it was Garrick who had their lovely rococo frames made for them. Garrick died in 1779, but his widow stayed on in the Thames-side villa and so did the Hogarths. She used to tell the story of how Garrick had bought them, and she liked to add that he never laid out his money to better advantage. She lived to be a very old lady and died only in 1823. The contents of the famous villa were sold and the 'Election' paintings went to Christie's. There was no lack of interest this time and the auctioneer's hammer came down at 1,650 guineas. 'As returning officer,' said the facetious ass in the rostrum, 'I have the honour of declaring that John Soane, Esquire, is the successful candidate in this warmly contested election.'

John Soane at this time was seventy years old and known to the public as an exceedingly distinguished architect and a somewhat thorny personality who collected antiquities and works of art at his very peculiar house in Lincoln's Inn Fields (No. 13). There he already had, among other things, Hogarth's 'Rake's Progress', which he had bought more than twenty years before. Apart from a marvellous Canaletto, a Watteau rather the worse for wear, a Turner, and a Reynolds, they were the only good pictures he had. Soane was not really a painting man. Architecture – the whole of architecture from the Greeks down to what was on his own drawing-board – was his lifelong obsession and there was not room for much else. Painting appealed to him, as it did to so many of his contemporaries, as primarily illustrative and anecdotal and that, of course, was why to possess Hogarths was, for Soane, to possess the best. To be Garrick's successor in owning 'The Election' was a triumph – something of a social triumph, I suspect, as well as a spectacular enrichment of the museum.

When the 'Election' pictures arrived at Lincoln's Inn Fields in 1823 there cannot have been room to hang them – the house was crammed – but Soane already had in mind the rebuilding of the house next door eastwards and the creation of a little gallery behind it. 'Gallery' is hardly the word: it is a room fourteen feet square (the size of an ordinary living-room) and very high, with skylights; and the walls open up like cupboards, with more and more pictures inside as one turns the tall wooden shutters. Here, on the outside of the shutters, the four 'Elections' were hung in 1824 and there they have hung ever since. The 'Rakes' came here also in 1824 from another part of the house but were concealed behind the shutters – I think because the scenes of debauchery and madness were considered rather horrid; today they hang in two lines right in front of you as you come into the room. So there are the early Hogarths – the 'Rake's Progress' of 1732 – in front of you; and the late Hogarths – 'The Election' of 1754 – two on each side.

But before you look at the Hogarths it is a good idea to glance upward to a canvas which leans out from the wall above the 'Rake's Progress'. It is an oil sketch by Thornhill, Hogarth's father-in-law, for a ceiling at Hampton Court. It has just been cleaned and it has a charm which Thornhill's finished works do not always have – a facile, but happy and sensuous piece of brushwork; one can understand how much Hogarth learnt from his familiarity with Thornhill's studio.

'A Rake's Progress' is just below. These pictures were cleaned seven years ago but, for technical reasons, very cautiously, and I think we must blame time and dirt for their relative dinginess, which rather takes the edge off their attack, their immediacy. Here is Hogarth, at thirty-five, exploring the dark innards of the town, watching, noticing, memorizing in the tavern, the brothel, the mad-house, and getting his results quickly on to canvas. What he achieves here – especially, I think, in No. 4, *The Arrest* – is the complete mastery of the animated group, the complex of six or eight figures all involved in one incident and all of them *really* involved, up to the neck. There are no 'properties', no old-masterish bits and pieces, to keep the thing going; and if the attitude of the Rake in this picture does look rather like the Apollo Belvedere trying to make a bolt from the Vatican, that is all part of the fun.

This mastery of the animated group was Hogarth's special gift, and in the twenty years after the painting of 'A Rake's Progress' it developed steadily. In the 'Election' pictures the astonishing thing is the unfailing double flow of invention – invention in anecdote and invention in painterly narrative. The anecdotes spill into paint just as the relation of a good storyteller spills into words, irrepressibly but with a due sense of whatever corresponds to 'timing' in a picture – 'spacing', I suppose: in other words design – narrative design. It is a curious faculty this, of narrative design, and one that has not much to do with design in the grand sense of filling a canvas with a powerful and indivisible composition. This was not a thing that Hogarth was very good at – he was even rather naïve in the way that he scaffolded his compositions. But after the scaffolding came the arabesque of anecdote and incident: stories capping each other, personalities in ludicrous contrast – fat people, thin people, funny people, people with poker faces – and so long as all these interested him Hogarth could weave their heads, bodies, and limbs, their garments, their bits and pieces into a continuously delightful design executed, especially in these late 'Election' paintings, with wonderful ease and fluency – and brilliant colour.

Let us stand in front of the first of the 'Election' series – that is, *The Entertainment* – and see what is going on. We have to admit at once that far too much is going on, a great many things that could not possibly be happening simultaneously. When a brick comes in through the window of a banqueting room and hits one of the diners on the head, people in real life are apt at least to glance in the direction of the injured diner. Nobody does here. Nor does it seem to bother anybody that the mayor has collapsed and is receiving medical attention or, indeed, that somebody outside is trying to break down the door. Everybody is involved in one specific episode and it is as a chain of episodes that the picture must be read.

It is not difficult. Let us start with Mr Abel Squatt, the Quaker in the green apron on the left, looking glumly at a suspicious I.O.U. (£50, payable at six months after date). A deft distribution of white linen leads from the Quaker to the next episode where one of the candidates, Sir Commodity Taxem, is being nuzzled by an old woman while her husband burns his wig with his pipe and a little girl removes his ring. (By the way, these names are attached to objects in the picture, but more legibly in the engraving than the painting.)

From here we move along the table – or rather tables; there are two, one oblong, one round, shoved together, just as would happen in a clumsily improvised banquet, and of course just what Hogarth needs to break up his episodes. At the oblong table we have two repulsive drunks, a cobbler and a barber, breathing on and pawing the second candidate; we have the fat sweating parson holding his wig; and we have a nasty little overdressed character stroking the chin of a fiddler behind him, an episode which spreads up into the group of musicians behind. Then at the round table we have some fine idiot faces watching the man who is reciting 'An old woman clothed in grey' with the traditional puppet-face drawn on the back of his hand; then comes the leech attending the collapsed mayor, then the man struck by a brick, and finally the warrior with the broken head who is being treated internally and externally with liquor and whose foot rests on the banner 'Give us our eleven days'.

That is not by any means all. Away back on the left an election agent is giving a present to a pretty girl while a tipsy lawyer shakes him by the hand and raises his glass. On the extreme right a puritanical tailor is being threatened by his wife for refusing a bribe, while his son points to the parlous condition of his shoes. And outside the window is a procession with an effigy labelled 'No Jews', and banners marked 'Liberty', and 'Marry and multiply in spite of the Devil'. Altogether there are thirty-four people in the picture, not counting some figures holding the door against intruders and the more or less indistinguishable crowd outside.

And what is it all about? Is there any sort of categorical message to be extracted from the picture? I hardly think so. Even when one has collected all the clues, pointers, and symbols, all they add up to is a declaration that electioneering is a thoroughly dirty business. Politically it is baffling because if the 'No Jews' mob outside are Tory (which they must be), the party inside ought to be Whig, and Whigs would hardly be sitting under a slashed portrait of William III. Or perhaps, in their ignorance and contempt of principle, that is just, in Hogarth's view, what they would be doing. From the human point of view there is no specific message because there is no contrast of vice and virtue. Both mobs, inside and out, are ignorant, stupid, drunken, lecherous, corrupt, and vain: all of them; the whole lot.

Hogarth's ridicule is wholesale and in all the thirty-four figures there is not one which has not some degrading trait: at least, I think not one. You can have it, if you like, that the woman fiddler perched up at the back is rather an old dear – but I doubt it.

It is impossible to explain these pictures in so many words. They represent great drafts on Hogarth's mental store of character and situation dramatized round the central theme of an election. The traditions preserved by Hogarth's commentators, J.B. Nichols and the Irelands, do not help much. It does not really help to know that Sir Commodity Taxem, the candidate who is having his wig singed, is supposed to be a portrait of a contemporary politician, Thomas Potter; or that the man reciting 'An old woman clothed in grey' represents John Parnell, a well-known Dublin attorney who suggested himself as a model because being so well known his face would help to sell the prints; or that the man squatting on the floor is Teague Carter, an Oxford bruiser.

No doubt if we could explore Hogarth's memory we should find that all the characters derive from real people whom Hogarth has at some time met or observed, just as the characters in a play may all have originals somewhere, though perhaps even the playwright does not know where. The great thing is that they are *characters* and this is the essence of Hogarth's gift. He really was an actor-playwright with a tremendous mimetic faculty; but for a whole variety of reasons the mimetics became diverted from the theatre into draughtsmanship and then into paint. Hogarth's satire is essentially theatrical satire, as distinct from the satire of caricature which rests on extreme distortion, or from literary satire which depends on the force of verbal arrangement. Hogarth's people are always mimed representations of the originals – never, or rarely, caricatures. They are human beings observed as an actor might observe them and represented as an actor might represent them.

This explains the apparent cynicism of much of Hogarth's work. He was not really a cynic or a misanthrope; he was a pugnacious individualist with a strong sense of social justice and a love-hate of the human animal. He wanted to mimic it and parade it like an actor,

56. Still-life detail from *The Entertainment*

and the actor in him went all out for the grotesque, the gnarled, the odd, the twisted – the types who seemed most to invite mimicry. It also explains the enormous and continuing popularity of Hogarth's work. Since his death eighteenth-century painting has had its ups and downs of esteem, but Hogarth's fame has never waned for a moment. The truth is that one does not have to know much about painting to be entirely and utterly captivated by Hogarth. His astonishing qualities as a painter as revealed in 'The Election' (and what other Englishman of the time could give us the brilliance of the still-life passages in *The Entertainment*? [56]) are only one aspect of his performance. Hogarth's place is as much in the history of English fiction and drama as in painting. He stands with Fielding and, as an heir of Shakespeare, with Garrick.

I sometimes wonder if Garrick's rather sententious little story of buying the 'Election' pictures out of a sense of friendship is entirely true. It was the story he told his wife when he got home. I cannot help feeling that in fact the great actor could not resist such a display of characterization. Over one hundred live characters in the four canvases: 200 guineas the lot. It was a bargain and, as Mrs Garrick used to say, 'he never laid out his money to better advantage'.

Neither, for that matter, did the prudent and judicious Soane, for I believe that more people come and have always come to his museum to see the Hogarths than anything else in the collection, which is in any case a small one and highly idiosyncratic. If you let your eyes stray from the Hogarths they will light upon Piranesi and Clérisseau, temples, tombs, pyramids. Open the shutters and you find Soane's designs for royal palaces and the Bank of England; open them again and you look down into the Monk's Parlour with its incrustation of gothic bric-à-brac and, beyond, a glimpse of a moss-green court with a make-believe tomb and ruined cloister. Tortuous, scholarly, dim, with strange shafts of beauty, the world of Soane encloses you as soon as you turn away from Hogarth. It is an unexpected setting, perhaps, for these illustrations of the robust, the crude, the depraved; but Soane and Hogarth have been together now for nearly one hundred and forty years, Soane offering us Hogarth in the severe, moralizing light which he and his age thought appropriate to the exhibition of such goings on.

*

Biographical note

William Hogarth was born in London in 1697. Only son of an unsuccessful schoolmaster and hack writer, he was apprenticed to a man who engraved ornaments and coats-of-arms. It was, he tells us, Thornhill's murals at St Paul's and Greenwich which awoke his interest in painting. He was, however, not only a born draughtsman but a born mimic. Whether he could ever have acted we do not know, but the draughtsmanship and the mimicry ran together into a genius of a peculiar kind which is the mainspring of his work. Very early he conceived a horror of academies and the copying of old masters; he looked for 'a shorter path'. In later years he wrote down what he remembered, as a youth, trying to do; it was 'to fix forms and characters in my mind, and instead of *copying* the lines, try to read the language, and if possible to find the grammar of the art by bringing into one focus the various observations I had made'. The key to this process was the 'technical memory' to which he attached the greatest importance.

Hogarth's career as a painter began with conversation pieces; they included scenes from Shakespeare and one from *The Beggar's Opera*. These theatre pieces led to something else. Why not, instead of representing a scene from a play, represent some scene from ordinary life *as if* it was in a play? And then, why not a series of such scenes, linked by a narrative and constituting a complete drama? The answer came in Hogarth's first cycle, 'A Harlot's Progress', painted about 1731. Hogarth himself engraved the pictures and the issue was successful. He promptly set to work on a companion series, 'A Rake's Progress' (now in Sir John Soane's Museum), showing the decline and fall of a rich young ass in the brothels and gaming houses of London. This again he engraved and published.

The 'Harlot' and the 'Rake' made Hogarth a celebrity. The next great series was the 'Marriage à-la-Mode' (1743), which hangs in the National Gallery. Then followed some of the most famous sets of prints – 'Industry and Idleness' (1747), 'Beer Street' and 'Gin Lane' (1751), and in the same year 'Four Stages of Cruelty'. In 1753 he published *The Analysis of Beauty*, written (says the subtitle) 'with a view to fixing the fluctuating ideas of taste'. Hogarth here reduces the idea of beauty to a set of principles, formally enshrined in the relations of a serpentine line to a pyramid or cone. The 'shorter path' again; the direct, commonsense view of how to achieve successful painting.

197

Then in 1754, when the painter was fifty-seven, came the four large pictures comprising 'The Election'. They formed his last series; he died in 1764.

History of 'The Election'

The impetus for the series was the general election of 1754, and, in particular, the county election at Oxford. Elections in the eighteenth century were usually adjusted on a basis of compromise between the county families. To fight an election was enormously costly and generally avoided. But it did sometimes happen, and it happened at Oxford in 1754, when the Whigs tried to capture this old Tory stronghold. From the end of 1752, battle was on. Among specific issues which served as targets for oratory was the 'Jew Bill', promoted by the Whigs – a wholly innocuous piece of legislation to enable foreign-born Jews living in Britain to obtain naturalization and thus the same rights as those who had been born here. 'No Jews!' exclaimed the Tories, and thousands of Englishmen who had never seen a Jew in their lives became rabid anti-Semites. Then there was the calendar. In 1752 Parliament had introduced the Gregorian calendar by the expedient of making 3 September into 14 September. What was this but a Whig atrocity, excising eleven days from the life-span of the common man? The political battle was finally decided at the hustings on 17–23 April 1754. The Old Interest won. Oxfordshire remained Tory.

Almost certainly it did not matter to Hogarth whether Oxfordshire remained Tory or not. One of the main things about the 'Election' series is that it is, in a sense, non-political – simply a portrayal of a number of human beings playing an idiotic game called politics. Hogarth was not, as we say, 'politically conscious'. The 'Election' contains not a scrap of party bias. Nor does it attempt to make specific reference to the Oxford election. The action appears to take place in a small country town, and we must conclude that the four scenes were conjured up out of Hogarth's whole experience of elections at various times and places.

57. Hogarth: *The Orgy* ('A Rake's Progress'). Sir John Soane's Museum, London

At the Soane Museum the series is seen alongside the 'Rake' series, painted some twenty-one years earlier. The latter are not only smaller but more diagrammatic in composition. Look at the scene from the 'Rake' whose subject-matter comes nearest to that of *The Entertainment*; it is *The Orgy* [57], where the rake and a lot of lewd women are round a table. The composition has the same basis as nearly all Hogarth's early paintings – a flattened pyramid with all the principal faces strung along its edges. Twenty-odd years later Hogarth still mapped out his canvases in much the same way, but with more subtlety. In *The Entertainment* the pyramid is still

199

58. Jan Steen: *The Prince's Birthday*. The Rijksmuseum, Amsterdam

present (its peak is the fiddle and bow in the hands of the old woman
in the background) but the faces are no longer strung along its
edges: here they seem to follow two bold s-curves sweeping up from
the foreground to left and right, in consort with the theory expounded
in *The Analysis of Beauty*.

It is impossible to look for long at *The Entertainment* without
being reminded of the Dutchman, Jan Steen [58]. A picture by Steen
in the Rijksmuseum at Amsterdam is a striking parallel to our
Entertainment. Painted almost exactly a hundred years before, it

59. *The Last Supper*: eighteenth-century engraving after Leonardo. The British Museum, London

shows a party of peasants gathered round two tables and celebrating the birthday of the Prince of Orange. Though there may be only a chance relationship between the two paintings, they are worth comparing if only because the gentle, ironic humour of the Dutchman and his elegant sense of composition emphasizes the merciless ferocity of the Englishman's crowded satire. Steen was certainly one of Hogarth's sources. And, of course, there are others. Some years ago Professor Wind pointed to a passage borrowed from Leonardo's *Last Supper* [59, 60]. No painter is absolutely original, but Hogarth

60. Detail from *The Entertainment*

bursts into the dreary scene of early Georgian picture-making with a point of view wholly his own. It was not strictly a painter's point of view, but that of a very singular man with a love-hate of humanity which drove him to describe most vividly the humanity he saw.

Books for reference

Antal, F., 'Hogarth and His Borrowings' in *The Art Bulletin*, vol. 29, March 1947, p.36

Beckett, R.B., *Hogarth*, 1949

Dobson, Austin, *William Hogarth*, 1907

Kurz, Hilde, 'Italian Models of Hogarth's Picture Stories' in *Journal of the Warburg Institute*, vol. xv, 1952, p.136

Hogarth, William, *Anecdotes of Hogarth, by himself*, ed. J.B. Nichols, 1833

Oppé, A. P., *The Drawings of William Hogarth*, 1948

Quennell, Peter, *Hogarth's Progress*, 1955

Robson, R. J., *The Oxfordshire Election of 1754*, 1949

Wind, E., 'Borrowed Attitudes in Reynolds and Hogarth' in *Journal of the Warburg Institute*, vol.II, 1939, p.182

Ascanius Shooting the Stag of Sylvia

Claude

Claude's enchanting *Ascanius Shooting the Stag of Sylvia* is almost his last picture, painted when he was eighty-two. But it shows no sign of weakness in dexterity of hand. Looking at it in the light of the whole sequence of his earlier works, one becomes aware that, for artistic as well as for poetic qualities, it shows him at the top of his form, and we are justified in detecting solutions to problems which the painter had been concerned with all his life, and in being prepared for almost any degree of subtlety. It is only in matters of administration and in dealing with other and younger human beings that people should be put on the shelf at sixty-five. In the field of vision, provided hand and eye still serve, you get enrichment rather than decay.

Consider the picture first as a landscape, without bothering about the story that the figures tell – not that the story is not also important for the all-over value of the picture as a complete work of creative art. What is the first impression one has from a quick glance? It is that there is a storm blowing up. Evening is coming on, and that sudden darkness which descends so quickly in Mediterranean countries will fall in a few minutes. A distant wind has begun to make itself felt. The sailing-boats far out to sea are already scudding in before a stiff breeze: in the middle distance, the man driving his mules over the bridge has already felt it and he is urging on the animals to the sheltering trees. It is felt also by the exposed shrubs in the centre foreground. But where the figures are, in a sheltered hollow below temple and hillside, there is still a pool of calm. The mood of the landscape and the mood of the history, of the story it tells, support one another. A storm is coming up, but the human figures do not yet know it: an action, the shooting of Sylvia's stag, is about to be performed, which will bring on another storm, the storm of war, of which the human actors are equally unaware.

Claude likes these stories from the second half of Virgil's *Aeneid* which bear on the mythical history of early Rome, but he always chooses a moment which is big with consequences for the future and not over-dramatic in itself. In the present picture he illustrates an action, innocent in itself, which had been contrived by Juno to stir up hostility between Aeneas and his Trojans, who have just landed in Italy, and the Latins who seemed about to welcome them. Aeneas's son, Ascanius, is made to shoot the stag – almost a tribal mascot – of Sylvia, the sister of one of the Latin rulers. This is the last straw which will lead to war. In another picture, one of the famous 'Altieri' Claudes, now belonging to Lord Fairhaven, Claude paints the next moment in the story – the arrival of Aeneas's ship at Pallanteum, just as Evander and his Arcadians are celebrating a national feast of great moment. This is the same kind of incident as the shooting of Sylvia's stag: undramatic in itself but suggestive of large historical consequences.

As well as taking place at a given moment in the story, the shooting of Sylvia's stag also takes place at a precise moment of a particular evening. We can tell where the wind is coming from and how far it has reached. It is a warm wind, bringing a good deal of moisture to the air. Claude's intention is to portray a fleeting moment. It is the same intention as the Impressionist landscape painters had. But the Impressionists were concerned only with what the eye can see in a single impression and with what the hand can paint of it. Claude is obviously concerned with something else as well, with the workings of the mind and of the imagination. He has arranged his landscape, however instantaneous the moment of time it portrays, in the interests of his story. But Claude acquired the mastery to do this by making drawings direct from nature in the same way that the Impressionists painted their pictures – drawings like that wonderful blobby dawn landscape of *The Tiber above Rome* [61] in the British Museum. He made a series of carefully studied compositional drawings as well for each of his pictures.

Normally Claude prefers moments of almost windless calm. His trees then have a dark central core and the leaves are painted in detail only at the edges of the general tree-masses. But the tall trees on the left in this Oxford picture seem almost to have been lightly

61. Claude: *The Tiber above Rome*, wash drawing. The British Museum, London

stippled on to the sky, and they achieve an effect of feathery movement which we are more accustomed to find in lithography. There is
something like it in George Stubbs's paintings on enamel. This is one
of the subtleties Claude had hardly attempted before.

An arranged landscape composition is a sort of box full of earth
and sea and sky into which the spectator is looking, and the front
side of which must be the picture plane. In a classical composition,
that is to say a composition in which a lucid order prevails and there
is a marked beginning and end to the design – as there is not in an
Impressionist picture – the matter within this box is broadly conceived going back in a series of parallel planes from the spectator;
and the view is closed by tall dark masses at either side (or towards

either side) of the picture. There are also one or two openings between these masses to allow the eye to explore the distance. But the chief technical or formal or visual problem – whatever you like to call it – in all Claude's pictures, what he was mainly concerned with all his painting life, is varying and diversifying what goes on inside this box so as to enrich the visual interest. He was the most single-minded of painters. All his life he painted only pictures of one kind: classical landscapes. But he achieved as much variety within this limited field as other painters whose repertory includes history and portrait as well as landscapes.

The horizon, of course, has to be a line parallel with the picture plane. It is the far side of the box. The rules of classical order require a certain number of other accents parallel with the horizon and the front plane; but interest and variety and a much greater sense of space and embracing air are best achieved by movement inwards, in the opposite direction. The problem which seems to have fascinated Claude especially was to reduce to the minimum his very decided parallel planes, to give the maximum of movement inwards in all directions, and thus to achieve in small section something of the endless movement of nature. But the finished result must be firmly held together within the picture frame as a visual unity.

Claude artfully sets his horizontal accents which bind the scene together into a classical whole by one visible line (by only one really) and by one invisible line. More or less in the centre of the mid-distance is the bridge, marking a road which traverses the picture-space parallel to the picture plane. That is the visible line, even though it is only a minute stretch of a straight line. The other line is marked only by the drawn arrow in Ascanius's bow. But it is clearly going to shoot straight across the picture at the stag and produces an equally compelling horizontal accent. These two straight lines, each not more than an inch or two long, hold the design together and make it seem to us that the viewpoint from which we are looking at this extensive stretch of land and sea is the inevitable one.

If you think the figures away, this piece of landscape also becomes more or less unmeaning – and this makes the point that the figures, and what they are doing, are of great importance in Claude's pictures. Those who believe that the value of a picture lies purely in what the eye can see, and is wholly independent of any story that it may tell, have suggested that Claude was not interested in his figures and their actions. But in fact the mood of his landscapes is dictated by the figures and I would be inclined to bet that he never started a composition without taking thought first of what the figures were to be and what they were to be doing. They were to be the germ round which the most intricate landscapes were built, like that tiny germ of actual incident Henry James used to build his most elaborate stories.

The older Claude grew, the more daring he became in taking liberties with his classical landscape designs. Here, the land-and-tree mass at the left is disproportionately larger and heavier than that at the right, and the main weight of the latter is set back much further from the picture plane. Letting the eye be guided by the land alone, there appears to be a strong inward diagonal movement from left to right. But this is set off by another diagonal movement in the opposite direction by the river which creeps into the picture at the bottom right corner. This cat's-cradle effect of movement within the box enormously enhances the sense of space and airy distance, and the spectator's viewpoint is also deliberately ambiguous for the same purpose. He is at once looking from a point about on the same level as the figures in the foreground, and surveying the sea from a higher point of vantage. He sees more than he should: much more than an Impressionist painter would allow him to see: this again is the work of the mind and the imagination.

We can detect these subtleties easily once we begin to look for them, but they do not for a moment obtrude themselves. Claude's art genuinely does conceal the art which goes to its making, because its great aim is not at all a complicated one – it is not to produce an immensely complex picture which can only be understood by much intellectual effort. It is to produce a greater and greater sense of air and light and wind. There is no painter whose works give out such gusts of fresh air as Claude's do. Just as it is often considered that the aims of figure painting are to produce the most powerful illusion of actual form and mass, the aims of landscape for Claude are to produce the most powerful illusion of those feelings of delight which we naturally experience in front of a real landscape. But Claude knew perfectly well that this is not achieved by the mere imitation of what the eye can take in at a single glance.

It would be right to call Claude's landscape generally – and not only when the figures are taken from Virgil's *Aeneid* – a Virgilian landscape. Nothing like it had been produced before. It was an imaginative discovery as important for the way in which the European eye has looked at nature as the discoveries of Galileo or Newton have been for European science. It is a sort of ideal combination of sea and mountain and plain and woods, which makes the perfect setting both for the old Mediterranean stories of gods and heroes and for the idyllic life of a pastoral Golden Age; and by an easy transference the stories of the Old Testament can be appropriately set amid the same sort of landscape. For instance, the titles of some of Claude's pictures in the National Gallery (perhaps the finest set in the world) are *Cephalus and Procris*, *David at the Cave of Adullam*, *The Marriage of Isaac and Rebekah*, *Narcissus*, *The Embarkation of St Ursula*, and *Aeneas at Delos*. They are all heroic tales of long ago and demand for their setting a kind of landscape at once ancient and modern: full of history and yet quickening our fancy by being the same kind of landscape we know today.

With a certain naïveness Claude gives antiquity to his landscapes by temples or pillared porticoes which look as if they had been built by the ancient Romans. But they are modern also because they remind us (even today) of certain stretches of the Italian coast or of inland hills – the Alban hills or the Monti Lepini – which are still immensely rich both in ancient legend and in ancient remains. To savour Claude's pictures to the full, as those for whom he painted them savoured them, we must I think have been to Rome and Naples. But they have an absolute value independent of these associations by giving us mysterious information about the possibilities for beauty and order in the world of landscape. They are communications of a profound knowledge gained by a love of

62. Detail of figures from *Ascanius Shooting the Stag of Sylvia*

landscape and of drawing it which can hardly have been surpassed. We can hardly overestimate their influence on the way later generations of Western man have looked at landscape and tried to *arrange* it.

The pleasure grounds at Stourhead in Wiltshire have claims to be the most beautiful piece of artificial landscape in this country. The spectator walks round the edges of an irregular lake and sees, every few steps, a different scene which owes its arrangement to the principles of Claude's pictures. Perhaps no other artist has established laws of natural beauty from the study of the landscape of one country

213

and had those laws imposed with such astonishing success on the landscape of another; and, by an odd irony, the kind of landscape gardening which owes its origins to Claude and the Roman scene is now known in Italy as *giardino inglese* – 'the English garden'.

Last, a word about Claude's figures [62]. They are often considered a joke. Roger Fry once called them 'totally inadequate', and, in Claude's latest works, they appear unnaturally tall and slender. We can tell that this was deliberate from the fact that the composition drawings – such as the one in the Ashmolean for this picture – show them as sturdier or more robust. In fact Claude clearly went to great pains to avoid anything like characterization in his figures. That would have stolen something from the landscape – and yet, whatever is the subject-matter of the picture, we can always recognize what they are up to. With a little thought we can see what he had in mind. He was painting a landscape which was the ideal poetic setting for heroic tales of long ago: as we walk through the Campagna today we can still – sometimes – fill it with the ghosts of these stories. This is exactly what Claude has done. He has made the ghosts a little more visible to the naked eye than the fancy of the normal traveller would achieve, but not enough to transport us wholly from the present into the past. Nicolas Poussin was concerned with making the past live again, and those who bought his pictures belonged to a small class of very highly educated men. Claude's pictures were meant as reminders as much of the present as of the past, and they could appeal to everyone, whether highly educated or not.

It is in this way that they can fairly be called, according to the way we think of them, both 'classical' and 'romantic'. Their sharp focus on the incident portrayed, their balanced composition, and their wonderful faithfulness to natural appearances, enables the lovers of the finite and of clear statement to admire them as 'classical'. It was these qualities which made them so loved throughout the English eighteenth century. But the age of Wordsworth and Keats rightly detected other qualities as well in Claude's pictures, which we can feel sure were just as much a part of the artist's intention. They

63. Claude: drawing after the finished design of *Ascanius Shooting the Stag of Sylvia*. The Devonshire Collection, Chatsworth

are pictures of something which one would have thought it impossible to put into visual form, of what Virgil calls *lacrimae rerum*, which nobody has succeeded in translating but which means something like that mood of poetic sadness which scenes of natural beauty evoke by suggesting the passage of many centuries of human history.

*

Biographical note

Claude Gellée (1600–82) was born in Lorraine at Chamagne, south of Nancy. There seem to have been artists in his family, but he first found his way to Rome as a boy in the capacity of pastry-cook. His early biographer Sandrart, who knew Claude personally, relates that he found it hard to get a job and acted as houseboy and factotum to a rather eccentric painter, Agostino Tassi, who was glad of help in the studio as well as in the kitchen. Claude may have stayed ten years with Tassi, from whom he learned a good deal more than the mere craft of painting. For Tassi was a specialist of considerable experience. He had been involved in the preparation of stage scenery for the Court of Tuscany, which was the most advanced in such matters, and he was much employed in painting fresco panels of landscapes and seascapes, adorned with appropriate historical figures, on the friezes of various Roman palaces. His connexions were good, and Claude, as his helper, must have had the chance to see and study many of the major fresco decorations in Rome. Claude went back home in 1625, but the call of Rome was too much for him, and he was back there in 1627 and stayed for the rest of his life, making only extensive journeys in the wonderful countryside round Rome, which is still known throughout the world as the Campagna, as if it were the only, or the ideal, countryside in the Mediterranean. We can guess that he extended these journeys to the coastline north and south of Naples. This landscape and these shores, and their associations, legendary, historical, and poetic, are the sole subject-matter of his art. They provided an unending variety of pictorial and poetic material and he never ceased refining upon the formal language in which he expressed it. The Ashmolean painting is Claude's last word and maturest statement about what mattered to him most as an artist; and, except as an artist, we know very little indeed about Claude at all.

Ascanius – its story and its composition

It was quite literally his last work, painted when he was eighty-two years old, and signed and dated *A Roma 1682*. He was clearly con-

64. Claude: an early study for *Ascanius Shooting the Stag of Sylvia*. The Ashmolean Museum, Oxford

cerned about the actual story which he set in his landscape, for he wrote on the picture in Italian *The Story of how Ascanius shot the stag of Sylvia, daughter of Tyrrhus. Virgil Book 7*. It was a story of much dramatic import – 'the first cause of travail, and fired the spirits of the Tyrrhenian peasants to war', which was to lead to the victory of the Trojans under Aeneas and his son Ascanius, and to the establishment of the imperial city of Rome, whose past glories filled the air and engaged the eye at every turn in the landscape Claude loved

217

65. Thomas Hearne: engraving for Payne Knight's poem *The Landscape*. The British Museum, London

to study. It may be that we shall begin to understand Claude's poetical world most easily by starting with what may seem to be the least important element in the picture, the story told by the figures and the buildings. We realize, once we begin to reflect, that we are looking at two long-separated periods of history at the same time. The wooded slope on the left is crowned with the ruins of a temple which bespeaks a splendid civilization which has long fallen into decay: it is a ruin such as could be seen in the Roman Campagna in Claude's own time, yet the figures who inhabit this landscape are those who, by their present actions, are setting in motion the long series of wars

66. Claude: *The Enchanted Castle*, 1664. Christopher Loyd Collection

and historical events which were to lead to the foundation of that very Empire the evidence of whose decay we see around us. They are ghosts summoned from the past by the poetic imagination. We are not looking at anything remotely resembling a transcription of nature: we are looking at a work of conscious art.

In his study of nature direct from the model, Claude made wash drawings such as *The Tiber above Rome* [61], in which the visual impression of a fleeting moment of light is all that he is concerned with. He constantly drew the details of the Roman Campagna directly in this manner, until he knew by heart the very fabric of which such landscape was made and could re-create it to suit his own purposes with complete imaginative and structural consistency. He began with this 'impressionism' and went beyond it to construct a new landscape with rules of its own, as consistent a 'landscape of art' as that of Cézanne. It keeps firmly, however, to a certain truth to natural appearances, because it was employed in the service of a specific class of patron.

For Claude was an extremely successful artist. From the time he was thirty he was constantly employed in painting pictures for Popes and princes and for the grandest collectors of most of the countries of western Europe. He was as sensitive to ideas as he was to the fleeting changes of tone in the sky, and he lived in a society which had a passion for Antiquity to a degree which is hardly imaginable today. The Virgilian world of the *Georgics* and of the *Aeneid* was as real to his patrons as the world of the newspapers is to us today, and it was into this world that Claude's mind became naturalized. The puppet world of figures from Virgil, Ovid, Tasso, or the Book of Kings, was common property. What was original to Claude was the setting and the amount of research he had given to that particular patch of real nature which was the ideal material for his settings. It is difficult for us to judge today to what extent it is because of Claude that the scenery round Rome and Naples seems to us today the only natural setting for all the great legends of the Mediterranean world.

How jealous Claude was of his rights in his settings can be seen from his *Liber Veritatis* in the British Museum. In this, Claude made a record of each important composition, as he completed it, and he kept these records in chronological order. He died before inserting into the *Liber* the drawing of his last composition, but he had made one, now at Chatsworth [63]. There is a puzzle about this, as the drawing bears two dates, 1671 and 1678, both earlier than the picture itself – although it has the air of a drawing after the finished design, as may be seen by comparing it with what is certainly an earlier study for the composition, the drawing at Oxford [64]. The three drawings illustrated represent three of the many stages through which all of Claude's finished oil-paintings passed. The Oxford drawing shows a composition already far advanced towards perfection, but to which certain formal refinements are still to be added: the Chatsworth drawing is a record of an achieved composition.

The painting was sold from the Colonna collection about 1789–99, and then passed through a number of English collections, notably the Northbrook one whence it was sold in 1919; it was presented to the Ashmolean Museum in 1926.

Claude and English taste

Rather oddly, it may seem, it was the great English collectors of the eighteenth century who inherited the taste of Claude's patrons. An astonishing number of his greatest masterpieces found their way to England, although it was not till 1799 that the Ashmolean picture left the Colonna Palace in Rome (for which it was painted). Not content with buying these splendid memorials which reminded them equally of Antiquity and the Campagna which they had visited, many Englishmen sought to remodel their native landscape on the compositional principles which Claude had devised – as can be seen from an engraving for Payne Knight's poem *The Landscape* [65]. By 1800 the landscape of Claude had become part of the English visual inheritance. It had first been admired because it was 'classical', but it gained a new hold when it was discovered that it was also 'romantic'. No picture holds a more eminent place in the history of English poetry than *The Enchanted Castle* [66], painted in 1664 for the same Constable Colonna for whom the *Ascanius* was painted later. The sight of it for Keats was as the voice of the nightingale, that

> *Charm'd magic casements, opening on the foam*
> *of perilous seas, in faery lands forlorn.*

Books for reference

Kitson, M., and Röthlisberger, M., 'Claude Lorrain and the *Liber Veritatis*', in the *Burlington Magazine*, vol. CI, 1959

Pattison (Lady Dilke), Mme M., *Claude Lorrain*, Paris, 1884

Röthlisberger, Marcel, *Claude Lorrain*, New Haven, 1961 (with full bibliography)

The Resurrection: Cookham

Stanley Spencer

To the people who think that all important contemporary painting should be 'at the height of its time' it must be rather disturbing that one of the outstanding masterpieces of the first half of the twentieth century is Stanley Spencer's *The Resurrection*. This picture has absolutely nothing to do with the art of its time: Fauvism, Expressionism, Cubism, Futurism, Surrealism, and even Impressionism might never have happened. It could, in fact, have been painted at any moment in the history of art since Giotto [67]. It would not look out of place in the Flemish Primitive Room in the National Gallery, or as a companion to Uccello's battlepiece of *The Rout of San Romano*. It is like some Pre-Raphaelite picture that has strayed by accident into modern times, but, unlike the Pre-Raphaelites, it is inspired not by poetry or literature but by life.

It is this timeless quality that sustains our admiration when more fashionable masterpieces have become just interesting period pieces. Already Picasso's *Guernica* seems to have worn a little thin and does not mean for us today what it meant in the nineteen-thirties.

But although *The Resurrection* might have been painted at any time, it could only have come out of one place. It is a great English picture, and takes its place beside Hogarth's 'Election' series, and Constable's *Hay Wain*. It is, I think, the greatest picture painted by an Englishman since the death of Turner.

The Resurrection was started in 1923, when Spencer was thirty-one years old, and finished in 1926. He painted it in a small room over a public house in the Vale of Health, Hampstead. Outside was a fairground, and Spencer used to say that the only way he could ever get far enough away to see his picture as a whole was 'to have two pennyworth on the swings' and glimpse it as he shot by the window. He used to say that the fumes from the cooking below mixed into the paint and gave it a unique quality; and many years later when the Director of the Tate Gallery suggested that the picture needed a clean, Spencer was dead against it, as he felt this quality would be lost.

67. Giotto: *Christ Appearing to Mary Magdalen*, c.1306. Scrovegni Chapel, Padua

The picture was exhibited at his first one-man exhibition at the Goupil Gallery in 1927, and was purchased by the Duveen Fund and presented to the Tate Gallery. It caused a considerable stir, and although it was praised by some of the serious critics, it was violently attacked in the sensational press, where words like 'cynical' and 'sacrilegious' were freely used.

The Resurrection is a great piece of autobiography which can tell you more about its author and his immediate family than any self-portrait could have done. Here, on the Day of Judgement, set in an idealized Cookham churchyard [68] with a view of the river beyond, you may read something of his spiritual and earthly life, of his friends, and of his wife. She is the tiny figure in a dark dress holding a staff on the bank of the river; she is also the girl on the path on the

68. Cookham Churchyard: photograph

left smelling a flower; she appears again in the figure in white lying on the tomb underneath the porch [69]. Her brother, Richard Carline, is the man in the brown suit lying with his back to us on the tomb on the extreme left, and he figures again as the nude by the railing directly below the right side of the porch, while the other nude man looking out to the right is Stanley Spencer himself. He is also the man lying on the tomb at the bottom of the right side of the picture.

The innovator of an art movement need not necessarily have a great artistic personality; it is the *idea* which takes possession, not the man. Claude Monet is a case in point. But if a man is to succeed as a reactionary artist, as Spencer undoubtedly was (and I do not mean it in any derogatory way), then he must do so by the sheer

227

69. Detail from *The Resurrection : Cookham*

force and originality of his own personality. If he is wanting in this, his work must be either a pastiche of the better men who went before him, or at best dully academic. It is Spencer's personality which is his great strength.

Spencer's art was a complete expression of his personality. He was a little dynamo of a man, his mind teeming with ideas, and he expressed his personality equally in paint or in words. His vitality was enormous. I remember a few years back going to the private view of the Royal Academy early in the morning, and seeing him surrounded by a number of admiring listeners. I came back in the late afternoon to find him still talking with great animation to a still larger following – he had been going all day long. That evening I went down to Cookham, and he arrived at the house where I was staying, having travelled down from town after the exhibition had closed. He then completely dominated the conversation till the early hours of the morning, when suddenly he stood up and said he must go home as he felt a little tired.

In the last months of his life, after he had had a terrible operation, some students of the Royal College of Art, not knowing how ill he was, asked if they could bring him over from Cookham to Burghclere by coach so that he could tell them about his murals in the chapel there. To my surprise he replied that nothing would give him greater pleasure. Once again he talked marvellously, explaining every feature of the work to his young audience. He was like an inspired schoolboy. On their way back they stopped at a little place for tea, and suddenly, with great intensity, he said, 'Isn't it wonderful to be eating bread and jam?'

In his work, too, it is the intensity of his observation of ordinary everyday things that is remarkable. He could take a commonplace incident like the two men with ladders on their backs in the *Christ Carrying the Cross* in the Tate Gallery, and give it such a new look that we find ourselves saying: 'Yes, that *is* what a chap looks like when he carries a ladder – but what a strange and exciting pattern it makes.'

Spencer was fortified by great technical gifts. Not only was he a fine draughtsman, but a master of every technical device in the armament of a figurative painter. His picture of *The Resurrection* is constructed as rigidly as a work by Piero della Francesca or Poussin, all the numerous ingredients being brought into one coherent design in a thoroughly masterly manner.

The Resurrection is intensely three-dimensional. We feel very conscious of its depth. It is charged with a force which seems to radiate from a point beyond the bottom left-hand corner and spread right across the whole picture. You can see how this happens if you look at the almost geometric placing of the tombs on the left, the lid

70. Detail from *The Resurrection : Cookham*

230

of the open one, the dark shadows of the foliage down the side of the church, the clump of yews on the extreme right, the dark figure among the flowers in the foreground [70], and the placing of the tomb with its reclining figure on the extreme right-hand corner of the picture. The more subtle placing of the graves on the right side of the porch, which prevents the eye coming to a full stop at the principal axis; this – the apex of the composition – is formed by the arrangement of tombs leading to the porch with its flowered top, in the exact centre of the picture. By contrast the wall of the church and railing are placed horizontal to the picture plane, giving the design its needed stability.

Spencer made use of a curious method of work in his elaborate compositions which makes us stand amazed at the unity he achieved. Having done a drawing and transferred it in outline to the canvas, he started at the top left-hand corner, finishing each piece completely and never revising, finally ending at the bottom right-hand corner.

We had an opportunity at the Royal Academy exhibition in 1960 of seeing the great unfinished picture of *Christ Preaching at Cookham Regatta*, with vast strips of white canvas contrasted with portions completely finished. To have chosen this manner of working proves that he could completely visualize the picture as a whole before he started, even down to small details. The only other artist who had this remarkable gift was William Blake, but even he never concerned himself with such involved designs. In the Resurrection picture Spencer appears to have deviated slightly from this procedure by indicating the main tones very simply in a grisaille underpainting.

One does not think of Spencer as a colourist, but in this picture his colour is masterly: the red blouse of the Negress below the porch sings out. The sense of tone and the handling of paint reach a plane which the artist never again achieved. After this he deliberately cut out the sensuous use of pigment and the strongly contrasted tonal qualities of his work. I do not mean to imply that his later work deteriorated; it changed its course and was to pursue a new and stony passage which led ultimately to the wonderful late flowering of his last picture.

71. Stanley Spencer: *The Resurrection: Port Glasgow*, 1947–50. The Tate Gallery,
London

It is interesting to compare this picture of *The Resurrection* with
the later version painted between 1947 and 1950, which also hangs in
the Tate Gallery [71]. The later work, with all its involved rhythmic
structure, seems turgid by comparison. There is no landscape to
relieve the eye from the writhing hordes of figures; we feel over-
whelmed, and rather repulsed. These are not the doll-like people of
the early work: 'I lost my innocence,' Spencer used to say. It was
only in the last few years of his life that he seemed to find serenity,
and in the final phase it is a change of mood, and not any change of
style, that becomes evident. It was to him Paradise Regained.

But it is the mood, the Spencerian quality, which really makes
this picture a great work. It is full of contradictions, and yet it has
unity. The setting is painted with realism, the flowers, the ivy, and
every blade of grass is treated with almost Pre-Raphaelite attention
to detail, and one would expect the figures to be painted with similar
meticulousness. But in fact it is peopled for the most part by doll-
like figures very much simplified, except where he introduces his
friends, or his wife, or himself, where he allows himself to be much
more naturalistic, and so there are two human species peopling the
same picture.

It is by this contrast of the figures and their setting that he makes
his effect of shock. How insistent he is to show us everything in his
beloved churchyard, the carving on the tombs, the texture on the

side of the church wall – the railings: 'It is here,' he seems to say, 'where we know every stick and stone, that this extraordinary thing takes place.' Out of their graves come these strange archaic people in their fantastic burial clothes, and languidly look around them at the old world.

He takes extraordinary liberties with the scale: look at the tiny people among the huge gravestones just below the river. To me this is one of the most eerie and imaginative passages in the whole work. It reminds me of another Spencer picture, one of the mural panels in the Burghclere Chapel. In it there is a crowd of wounded soldiers with their arms in slings which make innumerable white triangular patterns, and as one's eye travels through the crowds towards the distance, the triangles change from slings into angels' wings.

A similar incident occurs in *Christ Carrying the Cross*, where the fluttering curtains make wings for the onlookers who peer out from the windows. It is this illusory quality I find most fascinating of all in his work; Giotto had it to an even greater degree.

There are many things that excite, and some that puzzle me, in Spencer's *Resurrection*. What, for instance, is the significance of the children looking out of the tomb, whose hair is being firmly pulled by the dark figure behind them, or the strange group of black people, or the rather horrific men rising up with graves on their backs?

But there are also the gentler things to look at: how beautifully he manages the soft shadows that pass over the scene, and how luminous they are, and how marvellously nostalgic the tiny glimpse of the river with the sunlight flickering on the water.

I began by saying that this is one of the great pictures of the first half of the twentieth century. I do not know if I have succeeded in making my claim – and in any case 'great' is an impossible word to define. Perhaps it has something to do with individuality: and Spencer had that, he was truly an eccentric, outside the current of his time: but, beyond that, his *Resurrection* possesses what I think all great painting must have, some of the qualities of a symphony – its scale, its unity of purpose, and its ordered complexity. Ours is a period of

72. Stanley Spencer: *The Apple Gatherers*, 1912. The Tate Gallery, London

little works, and there are few people today whose art has the staying power for anything on this scale. Perhaps Ensor's *Christ Entering Brussels* possessed it – but even this seems superficial in comparison with *The Resurrection*. Like a great novel, this is a picture to which you can return again and again, always finding new treasures; and for me, at any rate, there is nothing like it in the world.

*

Biographical note

Stanley Spencer (1891–1959) was born in Cookham, bred in Cookham, and in Cookham he died. His father had been a church organist there, and the stiff stone angels, white tombstones in deep grass, the chest-nut trees dropping their flowers among the swans on the river, became the fabric of his vision. In the clear and complex rhythms of his painting there is an echo of Bach played on the organ of Cookham Church.

He began his career as a painter at Maidenhead School of Art, and when he was nineteen he went to the Slade School, where he went on painting the people, divine and human, who walked about in Cookham churchyard, until the First World War swept him off to Macedonia as a medical orderly in the R.A.M.C. There something very strange happened to him. He got a new vision, something – panic perhaps – in the Macedonian hills. The peace of Cookham had been shattered and not until he was an old man did he really begin to find it again. He came home from the war and continued painting, but it was not the same. Looking back from 1955 at what was happening to him then, he wrote:

Before the 1914 war I had to be very convinced about a picture before I drew it or painted it [72]. *The drawing or painting of the thing was the experiencing of Heaven.... This state of sureness continues to about 1922–3, when I did* The Betrayal. *At this time I did a series of drawings for the Burghclere Memorial and also the drawing for the 1927* Resurrection. *So that all the painting I was to do from 1922 to 1932 was settled in nearly every detail: ten years of solid bliss was ahead of me. But I knew in 1922–3 that I was changing or losing grip of something.*

His picture of *The Resurrection* in the Tate Gallery was painted between the years 1923 and 1927. Of it he wrote:

I was, I feared, forsaking the vision and I was filled with consterna-tion. All the ability I had was dependent on that vision. I knew of this in 1922–3 but I felt and hoped that having been able to do the Resurrec-tion *drawing and the Burghclere drawings that while carrying out this work I might recover my vision.*

But the earth is beginning to heave, the graves of Cookham

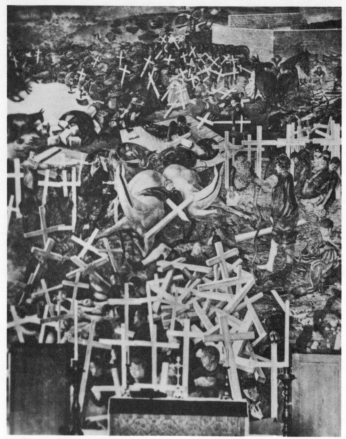

73. Stanley Spencer: *The Resurrection of Soldiers*, 1928–9. The National Trust, Burghclere Chapel, Berkshire

churchyard are giving up their dead and many strange things are about to rise with them.

Almost at the same time he was painting *The Resurrection of Soldiers* in Burghclere Chapel, soldiers carrying their crosses, and beyond them that disturbing, unforgotten Macedonian landscape [73]. The chapel at Burghclere in Hampshire had been built by Mr and Mrs Louis Behrend to commemorate their relative, Harry Willoughby Sandham, and here it was that Spencer executed what is perhaps one of the greatest pieces of European mural painting of the last three hundred years. When it was finished his fear seemed to come true. It was as though a dream had left him; the angel had come to earth. Perhaps it was the very intensity of his early purity which made the disillusionment of his middle period almost unbearably earthy. The people of Cookham were still there, but apostles and angels no longer walked among them. Girls with fat legs shrieked and giggled, people gossiped, shoved; their faces grew red, their eyes goggled, and they sweated. Sometimes the vision seemed to come back. He certainly struggled to regain it for he wanted when he had finished the Burghclere work 'to do not a chapel to do with war, but to do with the more vital meaning of peace'. Peace, however, had left him; perhaps he was trying to do too many things at the same time. Of this period he wrote:

This change in my work only becomes more glaringly apparent in 1932–3 because up to this time I was only carrying out what had been done in 1922–3. I recovered partly from this loss and in 1933 the next 'chapel' (built also in the air as was the first, the Burghclere chapel: that is to say not commissioned) was to be planned somewhat thus: the Village Street of Cookham was to be the Nave and the river which runs behind the street was the side aisle. The Promenade of Women, *and the* Sarah Tubb and the Heavenly Visitors *and the* St Francis and the Birds *and* Villagers and Saints *are fragments of the street scenes.*

No two men would have understood each other better than St Francis and Stanley Spencer, and yet, because the vision was leaving him, he did not paint the 'Little Poor One of God' with the heavenly intuition of his earlier work. He made him extremely fat, which shocks some people, although he said that by it he meant to signify, not a fat friar, but that 'the teachings of St Francis spread far and wide', a piece of naïve symbolism which the Poverello would no doubt have appreciated. In 1939–40 he painted a series of small

74. Stanley Spencer: *Christ Preaching at Cookham Regatta*, 1952

paintings of 'Christ in the Wilderness'. One of them, *The Scorpion*, is a strange picture.

> *Behold I give unto you the power to tread on serpents and scorpions, and over all the power of the enemy; and nothing shall by any means hurt you.*

Far from treading the scorpion under his feet, Christ holds it in the palm of his hand, watching it with a sort of calm curiosity while it curls its tail to sting him. The huge hand will no more crush the creature it has made than it would restrain Judas from going out to betray him. It is almost as though he were waiting to see what the

238

little beast will do. Perhaps that was how Spencer really regarded the things he had been trying to unearth in his *Resurrections*.

During the Second World War, he worked as an official war artist and executed a series of paintings in the shipyards of the Clyde, wherein the colour is so metallic that one can almost smell the sizzling paint. In 1952 he returned to the river aisle of his 'chapel in the air' with a series of paintings of Christ preaching at Cookham Regatta. Some time in the late 1950s they dug up the drains in Cookham High Street. Spencer was meditating a Crucifixion at the time. He wrote how he saw in the mounds of earth thrown up along the High Street a range of barren hills which seemed the right setting for the Passion of Christ. His last picture of Christ preaching at Cookham Regatta was a very great and complex painting [74]. Christ was sitting among his apostles in a wicker chair, with a boater on the back of his head, preaching to the astonished people of Cookham. It was not, however, a peaceful scene; his gesture seemed to promise not peace but a sword. Then, before he had finished it, Stanley Spencer laid down his brushes and went to find the vision for himself.

Books for reference

Newton, Eric, *Stanley Spencer*, Penguin Books, 1947

Rothenstein, Elizabeth, *Stanley Spencer*, 1945

Wilenski, R. H., *Stanley Spencer*, 1924; Introduction to *Stanley Spencer: Resurrection Pictures (1945–1950)* (includes notes by the artist), 1951

Stanley Spencer, Catalogue, Retrospective Exhibition, the Tate Gallery, London, 1955 (with an introduction by the artist from which most of his statements quoted above are drawn)

Sources of Illustrations

The Publishers wish to make acknowledgement to the following, who have given permission to reproduce works in their care:

The Wellington Museum, London, Velázquez, *The Water Carrier of Seville*; The Prado, Madrid, Velázquez, *The Adoration of the Kings*, *The Infante Don Carlos*; The National Galleries of Scotland, Velázquez, *Old Woman Cooking Eggs*; Stephen C. Clark Collection, New York, Cézanne, *The Card Players*; The Louvre, Paris, Caravaggio, *Olaf de Wigancourt*, Watteau studies, Corot, *The Sèvres Road*, Pissarro, *La Route de Louveciennes*, Holbein, *Niklaus Kratzer*; The Trustees of the Wallace Collection, Watteau, *The Music Party*, *The Music Lesson*; Städelsches Kunstinstitut, Frankfurt am Main, Watteau, drawing of Nicholas Wleughels; The Trustees of the National Gallery, London, Pollaiuolo, *The Martyrdom of St Sebastian*, *View From Louveciennes*, Hobbema, *The Avenue*, Duccio, *The Virgin and Child with Angels* (triptych), *The Transfiguration*, Masaccio, *Virgin and Child with Angels*, Tintoretto, *The Origin of the Milky Way*, Holbein, *The Ambassadors*, El Greco, *The Adoration of the Name of Jesus*, Mantegna, *The Agony in the Garden*; The Trustees of the British Museum, London, Pollaiuolo, *The Battle of the Ten Nude Men*, Claude, *The Tiber above Rome*, print after Leonardo's *The Last Supper* (artist unknown), Thomas Hearne, landscape engraving; The Bargello, Florence, Pollaiuolo, *Hercules and Antaeus*; Ehemals Staatliche Museen, Berlin, Botticelli, *St Sebastian*, Tintoretto, drawing for *Venus and Vulcan*; The Earl of Derby, Poussin, *The Gathering of the Ashes of Phocion*; The Metropolitan Museum of Art, New York (bequest of William Church Osborn, 1951), Pissarro, *La Côte du Jallais à Pontoise*; Musée Marmottan, Paris, Monet, *The Train in the Snow*; Accademia, Venice, Tintoretto, drawing after *The Origin of the Milky Way*; Alte Pinakothek, Munich, Tintoretto, *Venus and Vulcan*; Scuola Grandi di San Rocco, Venice, Tintoretto, detail from the *Temptation of Christ*; Isabella Stewart Gardner Museum, Boston, U.S.A., Titian, *Rape of Europa*; The Trustees of the National Maritime Museum, Greenwich, terrestrial globe; The Trustees of the National Portrait Gallery, London, perspective portrait of Edward VI (probably by G. Stretes); The Escorial, Madrid, El Greco, early version of *The Adoration of the Name of Jesus*; Casa Greco, Toledo, El Greco, *View of Toledo*; The Galleria Estense, Modena, El Greco, *View of Mount Sinai*; Reproduced by gracious permission of Her Majesty the Queen, Mantegna, *The Triumph of Caesar*; The Brera, Milan, Mantegna, *The Mourning over the Dead Christ*; The Trustees of Sir John Soane's Museum, Hogarth, *The Entertainment*, *The Orgy*; Rijksmuseum, Amsterdam, Jan Steen, *The Prince's Birthday*; The Visitors of the Ashmolean Museum, Oxford, Claude, *Ascanius Shooting the Stag of Sylvia* (two works); The Trustees of the Chatsworth Settlement (The Devonshire Collection), Claude, drawing after *Ascanius Shooting the Stag of Sylvia*; Mr Christopher Loyd (City Museum and Art Gallery, Birmingham), Claude, *The Enchanted Castle*; The Trustees of the Tate Gallery, London, Spencer, *The Resurrection: Cookham*, *The Apple Gatherers*, *The Resurrection: Port Glasgow*; The National Trust, Spencer, *The Resurrection of Soldiers*; Scrovegni Chapel, Padua, Giotto, *Christ Appearing to Mary Magdalen*; The Mansell Collection, Holbein, *The Arms of Death*.

Acknowledgements are also due to holders of artists' copyright for permission to reproduce works and to those who have given permission to reproduce copyright photographs:

S.P.A.D.E.M., Monet, *The Train in the Snow*; The Trustees of the Tate Gallery, London, Spencer, *The Resurrection*; Arthur Tooth & Sons, Spencer, *The Apple Gatherers*, *The Resurrection: Port Glasgow*, *The Resurrection of Soldiers*, *Christ Preaching at Cookham Regatta* (works). The Mansell Collection, Velázquez, *The Adoration of the Kings*, *The Infante Don Carlos*, Caravaggio, *Olaf de Wigancourt*; Pissarro, *La Route de Louveciennes*, El Greco, early version of *The Adoration of the Name of Jesus*, *View of Toledo*, *View of Mount*

Sinai, Mantegna, *The Mourning over the Dead Christ*, Corot, *The Sèvres Road*, Pollaiuolo, *Hercules and Antaeus*, Giotto, *Christ Appearing to Mary Magdalen*; Zoltan Wegner, Tintoretto, *The Origin of the Milky Way*, El Greco, *The Adoration of the Name of Jesus*, Mantegna, *The Triumph of Caesar*, Hogarth, *The Entertainment*, Spencer, *The Resurrection: Cookham*, Pissarro, *View from Louveciennes*, Holbein, *The Ambassadors*; Professor Talbot Rice, wall paintings, *The Nativity*, *The Last Judgement*; The Arts Council of Great Britian, Monet, *The Train in the Snow* (photographs).

B.B.C. Home Service: 'Painting of the Month'

The talks on which this book is based were taken from the first two years of a series of B.B.C. educational broadcasts. These are linked with a scheme for subscribers who receive coloured reproductions of the works discussed, together with background notes and other illustrations in black and white.

Since its inception in 1960, 'Painting of the Month' has continued to develop and experiment. In 1962, the paintings in each quarter were of a particular *genre* – still life, figures, portraits, and landscapes. The 1963 series contained twelve Renaissance masterpieces – from early painters like Sassetta to the monumental art of Michelangelo, Titian, and beyond.

In 1964 the scope has been further extended: to the monthly talks on painting, a supplementary series has been added in which speakers discuss works of sculpture, architecture, ceramics, etc. As in previous years, all works discussed are on view to the public in Britain.

'Painting of the Month' (and now its supplement) has indeed contributed to listeners' enjoyment of painting, and extended their visual awareness. One listener wrote, 'It made all "looking" more interesting and I now find myself looking out for compositions when the bus stops along our country route or in the little towns. . . .'

Such letters are an encouragement for the future; and an affirmation of the intention of the series, which is, quite simply, 'enjoying paintings'.